MORE PREACHING
FROM THE
OLD TESTAMENT

By the same author:

Preaching on Special Occasions Vol. 1
Preaching on Special Occasions Vol. 2
Preaching through The Acts of The Apostles
Praying through The Christian Year
Have You Anything to Declare?
More Preaching from The New Testament

MORE PREACHING FROM THE OLD TESTAMENT

D.W. Cleverley Ford

MOWBRAY
LONDON & OXFORD

CONTENTS

ACKNOWLEDGEMENTS

This book is written in response to the invitation of the publishers, Messrs A.R. Mowbray & Co. Ltd, to follow my book *New Preaching from the Old Testament*, published in 1976 and now out of print; hence its title, *More Preaching from the Old Testament*.

I am indebted to Miss Hilary Mousley for permission to reproduce in Sermon Outline 24 the lines about Salisbury Cathedral written by her mother, Iris St Hill Mousley, and published in the *Sarum Gazette* of October 1958; and to Mrs J. Hodgson for preparing the typescript for the publishers.

Lingfield 1982   D.W. CLEVERLEY FORD

INTRODUCTION

In writing this book of twenty-six sermon outlines on the Old Testament I have tried to keep two basic principles in mind—to be true to Christian preaching and at the same time to be true to the Old Testament which is a pre-Christian book or collection of books. To hold these two principles together is not easy and this constitutes no small part of the problem of preaching from the Old Testament today. Students of theology will know of the various devices to which recourse has been made in the history of Christian Church to overcome this tension—allegorization, typology, the concept of progressive revelation—to name only three.

Preaching is essentially proclamation. It is not primarily designed to impart information or homiletical advice though it may involve these. The Bible sets the style in its opening words, 'In the beginning God...' The existence of God is neither argued nor explained. It is simply announced. This is not to say that there are no arguments in favour nor explanations of it, but they do not operate to build up a case for God. The Bible announces God's presence beyond and within the world and then proceeds to record what he says and what he does, using various literary forms in which stories figure frequently. Preaching is this kind of proclamation and Christian preaching must include as basic the proclamation of Christ even when preaching from the Old Testament.

As well as being true to Christian preaching I have tried to be true to the Old Testament. That is to say, I have tried to avoid a kind of Christian reading in what is not there. A clear example will be found in Sermon Outline No.17 called 'Touching bottom' based on the book called Esther. Esther is a bleak book and I do not think it is dealt with fairly by sifting the story to see if there can be found a comforting verse here and a comforting verse there able to be forced into a spiritual or Christian application. Far better not to preach from the book at all if we cannot use it for what it is—the record of a low water mark in the faith of God's chosen people.

I have used some of the personalities of the Old Testament for sermons—Absalom, Obadiah, Jonah—they abound in the various books. A preacher deprives himself of some of the most colourful and powerful sermon material if he makes no use of these. He must remember, however, that the ancients were not interested in personality as we are, and certainly the aim of the biblical writers is not primarily to provide a gallery of human portraits. Its overall aim is to make God known to us in and through life as we experience it, and the preacher will not be fulfilling his ministry unless he makes use of personality presentations to this end. I hope my attempts in this field will pass this test.

I have arranged the contents of this book in the order in which the books of the Bible occur with one exception. This is the last sermon outline called 'Morning has broken'. The reason for this is that I wanted to give some impression of the magnificent unfolding story of Israel's religion and how it eventually runs out, but the running out is not the end, the light of Christ is the new dawn, and this surely is the subject *par excellence* for Christian preaching.

In this collection of sermons are some which develop theological themes but I have been careful not to present these in abstract form. In a large part of the Bible, and especially of the Old Testament, the message, or shall we say the word of God, arises out of the story told, and told brilliantly. The preacher who uses the Old Testament must learn how to retell those stories so that what was living once will be living again. Then the hearers will hear what they are able to hear. It may not be what the preacher either expected or intended. He should not worry. What he cannot do is control the word of God. It runs as the Spirit wills it to run. If the preacher remembers this he will avoid the disastrous pitfalls of the preaching ministry called indoctrination and authoritarianism.

Who is sufficient for preaching from the Old Testament?
I certainly question my own competence but I offer what I
have written in the hope that other preachers will succeed
where I have failed, because I firmly believe that the riches
of the pulpit will never be experienced if through fear or
misunderstanding this stirring part of the Bible is
neglected.

D.W.C.F.

1. The Maker's Labels

Genesis 2.7 (NEB) *Then the Lord God formed a man from the dust of the ground and breathed into his nostrils the breath of life. Thus the man became a living creature.*

I would not be surprised if we smiled at this text. It sounds old fashioned, unscientific, even childish, especially that piece about man being formed 'from the dust of the ground.' On the other hand, I would not be surprised if we shrugged off this biblical diagnosis of what a man is because the subject is too difficult, a matter only for specialists—but I wonder?

Shortly after the last war the idea of artificial insemination for humans began to be canvassed. AIH and AID it was called, and Church authorities thought it right to pronounce on the subject. Of course the practice was widespread in the selective breeding of animals with beneficial results, but is it right for humans?; if not, why not? And then, about 1970, genetic engineering became known to the public and is now very much in the news again; and the process called 'cloning.' Moreover, for some years, birth control, abortion and euthanasia have been much in the public mind, and are likely to remain so.

What attitude ought the Christian to adopt towards these practices? He can of course react emotionally against them, which, although understandable, is not helpful. He can evade them on account of their difficulty, for agonizingly difficult questions they certainly do raise. But is there no guidance available? Are there no maker's instructions for those who believe that God is man's creator? Does not the Bible provide some indication of how our minds should turn on these life and death matters? I think it does. It says, 'Then the Lord God formed a man from the dust of the ground and breathed into his nostrils the breath of life. Then the man became a living creature.' Before we dismiss the words as comic or primitive, we should hear what they say.

1 Man's glory

First and foremost, they tell us that man is God's creation; he is the product of God's fashioning. His is the name on the maker's label attached to his person.

This is not, however, how the scientific humanist views man. True, he grants him a lofty status. Man is the peak point of nature's evolutionary process. He has no rival. He is unique now in the universe. This being so, he is lord of the universe. He can control it, adapt it and improve it, including of course the human species; and all by the techniques his astonishing intellectual skill has devised. He does not derive from the hand of any Supreme Being, for none exists. And if he bears any label at all attached to his person, it bears the words, 'Product of evolution.'

When therefore we turn to the great questions of our day about abortion, euthanasia and genetic engineering, we must expect diverse views on the part of those who see man with God's name attached and those who only see the label 'Product of Evolution' attached. Our text asserts that man is a creature God has created, and not only created, but created in his, that is God's, own image and likeness, able therefore to have fellowship with him. Christians must weigh up the modern problems about man in the light of this, the maker's label.

2 Man's lowliness

Secondly, we note from out text that man is formed 'from the dust of the ground.' Whatever else this may mean, it certainly means that man has a very earthy side to his nature. If there is one sense in which he is like God, there is another sense in which he is very *unlike* God. For one thing, God is pure Spirit, and man possesses a material

2

body. Man is also a creature whereas God is the Creator. Man has therefore a humble origin and, in a way, an humiliating affinity with the animals. He is one, among others, of God's creatures. May we therefore believe (even if we cannot prove) that man is the product of some evolutionary process and this is what the phrase 'dust from the ground' implies? Yes, but not to believe it as the scientific humanist believes it. Christians cannot simply see the label attached to mean 'Product of evolution', he must also see the words attached 'Made by God in the image of God.' God is behind and within the evolutionary process in whatever way we are to understand it. This is the difference.

Perhaps in passing we should note that the concept of evolution as applied to man does raise a difficulty. Has man ceased evolving? Or will there be some super *homo sapiens* in some far distant future? When the scientific humanist cautiously shakes his head, his reason is that the structure of the human brain is such that it has no room for any further development. When the Christian shakes *his* head, it is because he believes that manhood reached its perfection in Jesus of Nazareth whom we call the Christ. Evolution *pure and simple* then apart from God's purpose, is not a thesis the Christian can accept.

3 Man's destiny

Are there any other maker's labels attached to man suggested by our text—'The Lord God formed a man from the dust of the ground and breathed into his nostrils the breath of life. Thus the man became a living creature.'? Yes, thirdly, we learn that man is a psychosomatic whole, a soul-body complex. He is essentially this, that is to say, he is this *in essence*, and without this soul-body complex he is not, he cannot be, a human being.

Let me elaborate. A human being is not in essence a soul which for a time inhabits a body as if it were some kind of tiresome, even if only temporary, abode. This view of what a man is derives from Greek thought, not from the Bible. It

3

has however been widely believed. And it has had two widely different results. One has been to mortify the body as an evil thing for ever dragging the soul down from its separate and elevated purity. The other, quite the opposite, has been to indulge the body to its full capacity because it is only the house which the soul occupies, anyway, and is doomed to destruction sooner or later, thus freeing the soul for its eternal destiny. A modern variant of this view is to see the body as a machine subservient to well-defined physical laws, and the soul, if such exists, as the ghost in the machine. Our text lends no credence to these views.

Neither does our text support the view that a man is his body, that is to say, his body is basic and from it every other part of him has developed. Mind, self-awareness and spirit, included maybe under the general name 'soul', have derived from the material body. They are an outcrop upon it, almost a parasitic outcrop; that is to say, although they now possess a quasi-existence on their own they derive from the body; the physical is prior to the spiritual and can be said to be fundamental. On this materialistic view, the essence of a human being is the chemical element, carbon.

What then does our text give us to understand? That a human being, similar to the animals in the possession of a body, though more complicated, also possesses a soul. Man is bipartite. There is the physical and there is the spiritual; but the spiritual does not exist, anyway, on its own, it is given for the express purpose of animating the material body, indeed, animating that *particular body* with which it is united. A human being is a psychosomatic whole. He is what he is because of his body *and his soul*, his soul *and his body*. We do not therefore in the Christian profession of faith speak about the immortality of the soul, but about the resurrection of the body. The destiny God intends for man beyond death is life in a spiritual body not unconnected with the present. Our destiny is not to be disembodied spirits. The body is an integral part of the whole.

So we come back to our modern problems. Can we do as we like with our bodies, or are there some treatments of the

4

body which in actual fact dehumanize the person? Are there some forms of genetic engineering which make the subject undergoing them less of an individual human being with distinctive characteristics? Is it right by surgery to alter personality? Ought man to engage in the manipulation of his own evolution? Ought he so to interfere in the normal birth processes that he brings about, or attempts to bring about, a race of beings, every one of which is a genius? Is selective breeding a thing of the future?

Who is there who will not face these as frightening questions? Who is there who will not be tempted to cry, 'Let nature take its course.'? But where would we be today without the adventurous strides medical science has taken to ease pain, correct deformities and generally enrich the quality of life? And who will complain if it becomes possible to avoid, for instance, the birth of mongol children with all the suffering this entails for both parents and child?

There are no clear cut and dried answers to be found in the Bible to these disturbing problems. Nor are we delivered by our Christian faith from using our brains to try and come to reasonable, as distinct from emotional, conclusions. Nor must we forget that because something can be done it does not necessarily follow that it ought to be done. Nor does the elimination of pain automatically justify a course of action. No, there are no short cuts to the finding of answers to our problems. But there are at least three maker's labels attached to every human being we must not ignore. This man is God's creation designed for fellowship with him. This man is an earthy creature probably open therefore to improvement and development. This man is not distinctive simply for his body or simply for his soul, but for the psychosomatic complex which he is essentially, and for whom there is an eternal destiny. Or in the words of my text, 'Then the Lord God formed a man from the dust of the ground and breathed into his nostrils the breath of life. Thus the man became a living creature.' Genesis, 2.7. If we think out our policies, neglectful of these maker's labels, we shall, I believe, go seriously astray. Please study the labels.

5

2. The Significance of Egypt

Exodus 1.8 (RV) *Now there arose a new king over Egypt, which knew not Joseph.*

I wonder if you have ever visited Egypt? Quite a number of men have had this experience through being in the army. But whether we have visited it or not, we all know about Egypt. You can't be a civilised person and not know about Egypt. Egypt is constantly in the news. The names of recent Presidents have been on everyone's lips—Nasser, Sadat, Mubarak. For much more than five thousand years Egypt has been in the news, and probably will be as long as life continues on this planet. It could scarcely be otherwise, because of Egypt's geographical position. Egypt is Egypt because of the Nile; and now there is Suez.

1   Egypt as an experience

The point I wish to make, however, is that you cannot have even a superficial acquaintance with the Bible and not know about Egypt. I do not mean to imply that to understand the Bible you need to be an amateur Egyptologist or even to have visited that remarkable exhibition of Tutankhamun's treasures loaned to the British Museum. It is certainly not necessary to read up the histories of the thirty-one dynasties of which Manetho tells us, or even the third and sixth dynasties when most of the pyramids were built (i.e. 2815–2294 BC). What you must know is Egypt *as an experience*. After all, it was not simply ancient history the Psalmist had in mind when he sang:

'When Israel came out of Egypt: and the house of Jacob from among the strange people,
Judah was his sanctuary: and Israel his dominion.'

6

Nor was it history when the negroes of the Southern States of America sang:

> 'Go down Moses,
> Let my people go.'

Egypt in the Bible stands for an experience, a human experience, a spiritual experience, an experience of crushing depression and an experience of such a delivery as gives a song in the heart.

2 Egypt in history

We do, however, need to give some attention to history for the simple reason that both Judaism and Christianity are historical religions; that is to say, God became known through events in history. And this is still true. We come to know God, not in a vacuum, but through the experiences of life. Maybe we can know *about* God through reading books, attending lectures, or even studying western architecture; but we cannot know God for ourselves until we encounter him in experience, and this probably will include 'Egypt.'

The Hebrew people were all but crushed in Egypt. It wasn't their last experience of the tyrant's jackboot, but it has become the archetype of all subsequent experiences of oppression. 'There arose a new king over Egypt, which knew not Joseph.' A former king had favoured this people because of the outstanding service Joseph, one of their number, had rendered Egypt in time of famine. But now xenophobia had taken over, and racial discrimination actuated by fear of an alien over-population. So this new king formulated his ethnic solution of the problem; he would crush these foreigners out of existence by slave labour and reap the benefits of their pains for the architecture of Egypt. So the store cities of Pithom and Raamses arose, pouring out the cheap blood of thousands upon thousands to accomplish it as in many other places in the world's history, not least the

Colosseum in Rome under Titus in AD 80 and St Petersburg in Russia under Peter the Great in 1703.

It was a terrible oppression in Egypt, so terrible there was no will left for revolt. Tyrants have learnt how to accomplish this. It is to starve people, debilitate them and emaciate them till they lack the physical strength to rebel, or even the mental agility to contemplate it. Russian Communists have perfected the methods. Read your Solzhenitsyn. Labour camps designed to crush, however, were invented long before Egypt used them. And there was no resistance. But that is not quite true. The Bible records an element of resistance, but not from the men. Two women resisted. Two midwives. They tricked the government by seeing to it that male children were not all drowned at birth as the law required. They risked their lives for this action.

3   Our bondage

Does this all belong solely to the history books? But has not the whole Church tasted the galling experience of suppression? There have been persecutions by Rome and Islam. Christianity, brought to Japan in the sixteenth century, was battered out of all existence by the most appalling barbarity. Twentieth century Europe experiences another kind of suppression in the suffocating dominance of materialism and secularism, which scarcely allow the life of the spirit or the hope of immortality to survive as reasonable options. Resistance is at a low ebb. The majority follow the fashion.

And what about individuals? Have we not known, many of us, the bitterness and bondage of frustration? A man or woman chained to an illness, or the incapacities of advancing years which will not permit the freedom to do what is desired? This is our Egypt. Or it could be unemployment. This can act as a scourge. Nor is the recession always to blame. Since the world began men and women have been rightly conscious of possessing gifts but lacking all opportunity to exercise them. Do not forget that for every artist who catches the limelight there are scores for whom the chance never came. That, too, for them is bondage in Egypt. And children with the disadvantage of a broken home, sometimes crippling. Others with a birthmark. There is no need to search beyond our own street for people suffering the Egyptian experience. But is there no way out of all this? Can life offer nothing better than the chained experience? Is there no exit? No exodus? Chapter one of the book called Exodus, from which my text was taken, ends with two of the most arresting verses in the Old Testament containing four significant verbs about God in relation to the oppressed in Egypt. God heard, God remembered, God saw and God took knowledge. In view of those four verbs we can expect something to happen.

4 The unexpected

But what happened was *un*expected. It is women again who occupy the stage. The men are left out at this most significant point in biblical history. An unnamed Hebrew woman bore a male child so attractive to the mother (but then aren't all children attractive to the mother?), that she could not bear to abide by the law and pitch him into the Nile; so she half obeyed it and committed him to the Nile in a kind of paper boat. But not at random. She put him where another unnamed woman might see him, Pharaoh's daughter—and yet another woman to hide and watch the outcome. Women are not inept at subtleties (they have good reason not to be), and this trick worked. The baby excited the maternal instincts of Pharaoh's daughter when he cried in his little boat, and, condemned Hebrew though she knew him to be, she nevertheless arranged for him to be reared and ultimately transferred to the Egyptian court.

We ought not to miss the flimsy hinges on which this giant hinge of world history is beginning to turn. A condemned baby in a paper boat on the mighty river Nile. A chance discovery by a tender-hearted woman. A child's cry. A trick which worked (but which could have failed), so that the child was suckled by his mother until sufficiently old to be claimed by the princess who discovered him. What course would history have taken if the child had not cried at the moment he did, revealing his existence? But then over and over again history has turned on flimsy hinges.

The point of overriding importance which the Bible makes is that God was at work here; and then the state of the hinges on which the events turn simply does not count. Never despise the apparently trivial in your life. You never know . . .

So Moses was born (the name means 'drawn up out of the water'), reared and educated in the court whose culture and civilization were the flower of that ancient world. Josephus, with perhaps an understandable exaggeration, has written that he was so tall and so beautiful, passers-by used to leave their occupations to gaze at him. This was to be Israel's deliverer, God's leader, for bringing the Hebrews out of Egypt, out of 'the house of bondage.'

5 The man who delivers

We need to note from all this *how* God delivers his people from oppression. We cannot expose here the whole story of the Exodus (as that delivery or rescue operation is labelled in the Old Testament), but we can observe certain salient points.

God delivers his people from oppression by *human agencies*. It was not first of all a philosophy that God provided, by means of which the people would free their spirits and so themselves, nor even a theology, much less a political theory, but a person, an outstanding man—Moses.

We also need to note that that leader was one of themselves. He was a Hebrew, a Hebrew who identified with his brethren, but he was not restricted to their level of culture or intelligence. He was nourished and trained in Egypt. Apparently not even God can bypass, for the production of his agents, culture such as the world can provide.

10

Thirdly, we should not overlook the significance in this story of the two abortive attempts Moses made to avenge wrongdoing, committed first upon, and then by, one of his brethren. Those attempts failed in their purpose because they were carried out on impulse by one who as yet lacked both calling and rank for leadership.

All this points, not to ministry on behalf of God's oppressed people as an abstract thing, but to ministers who are persons of quality, set apart and authorized to plan and effect what needs to be done.

And further still, it points to one who, in unique fashion identified with his people, but yet stood apart from his people—Jesus of Nazareth. His infancy, like that of Moses, was risked under the murderous intent of jealous King Herod, and in an outhouse with no hygiene. But flimsy hinges do not baulk God's purposes. This Jesus is the Christ who sets us free.

Free from what? Free from ourselves to be ourselves. Free from fear of the future, for we are his. Free from the bondage of resentment at what life happens to have dealt to us, because, by the grace of God, something can be made of it, as ten thousand lives have shown in the pages of Christian biography. Egypt is the experience of frustration most of us know; but Egypt as a place of deliverance we can also experience, if we do not choose to turn down the man whom God has provided, Jesus Christ our Lord.

3. God's Name

Exodus 3.13 (JB) *But if they ask me what his name is, what am I to tell them?*

There must be very few people wholly unaware of the confusing experience of being unable to put a name to a face. A short time ago someone on the sound radio (I cannot remember his name!), recounted this experience of sitting

11

opposite a man in a train and not liking to ask his name because he ought to have known it. So he produced his passport making the comment, 'Funny how these photographers always make us look so ugly!', expecting the other man to produce his as well and then he could read the name and extricate himself from his predicament. But the ruse did not work. All he said was, looking at the photograph, 'Well, I can see who it is!'

1   The significance of names

Names *are* important, even with us Europeans, but nothing like so important as with men and women of the Bible. In our culture, a teacher in a class is much more effective if he can say, not, 'You there in the red jersey, what is the answer?', but, 'John, what is the answer?' A name establishes personal identity, and with it some admission of personal worth. Moreover, this small effect has a curious way of building up. If I am rather fond of a girl called Mary, every time I hear the name Mary I experience a pleasant sensation. My first (I say first) reaction might even be to approach all Marys warmly.

Names count; for the men and women of the Bible they are of deep significance. A name may imply character—so Peter means rock-like man. Or a name may indicate what the parents felt about the child when he was born—so Samuel means, 'I asked the Lord for him.' Or a name may even be given as a witness to a prophet's message. Isaiah called his son Maher-shalal-hash-baz (poor little boy!), which means, 'Speed-spoil-hasten-plunder.' When then the question is asked, what is *God's* name, what was really being sought was knowledge of God's *character*, and what he will do for his people. What God is, is shown by what he does.

2   The key scripture about God's name

This concern to know God's name is the key point of the passage in the Old Testament which has probably been studied and commented on more than any other. I refer to the incident of the bush in the desert astonishing Moses because it burned but was not consumed.

In itself there was nothing all that unusual in a dry thorn bush going up in flames in the scorching desert heat. The sun's rays could be concentrated by a fragment of quartz acting like a burning glass. There was however something very unusual in the flames not leaving the bush a charred residue of tangled wood. Nor was there anything unusual about Moses leading his sheep through the desert in search of pasture, it was a routine he had followed day after day with humdrum regularity since he had sought to identify with his Hebrew brethren. But the commonplace became for Moses the utterly unique. God gave an intimation of his name. He also summoned Moses to be his instrument for delivering his people from the slavery of Egypt. And this event now recorded in the Bible has intrigued myriads of people for hundreds and hundreds of years.

3   The teaching of this key scripture

What does the story tell us as it has now come down to us in the book called Exodus?

(a) First, that God is not a Being whom we discover, but *a being who reveals himself.* God is not a product of research but an unexpected, sometimes even unwanted, intrusion upon our routine. And because all the initiative is taken away from us in this matter of knowing God as a present reality, we cannot boast of our faith. It is a gift and not an acquisition, a surprise and not an achievement. And as a result God is sovereign and we are subject. He is the Lord and we are the dependents. This being so, we have no control over where and when and how we may come to know God for ourselves or cause other people to come to know God for themselves, not even our children. The most we can attempt is to place ourselves and others where we have learnt that God has revealed himself in the past. God may use so-called appointed means, or he may not. Isaiah encountered God

13

as a living reality in the temple at Jerusalem, but for Moses it was a burning bush in the desert, and for Amos a common almond tree in blossom.

In a book entitled *Amazing Grace* by John Pollock (Hodder and Stoughton, 1981), there is set out in gripping fashion the sordid story of John Newton's life as a slave trader, ending in his becoming a Church of England clergyman and author of the hymn, 'How sweet the name of Jesus sounds in a believer's ear.' It is impossible not to be revolted, if not numbed, by the all but boring record of cruelty for which he was responsible in transporting the blacks from Africa to the West Indies, and the lust which found no barriers in this man to prevent him from taking what naked black women he wished from the ship's hold on successive journeys, for his own satisfaction. But God became real to him and changed him utterly. The secret was what in a way is a very common and ordinary thing—his love of a Christian girl in England in his youth, called Polly, which had never died. Through that attachment God made possible for John Newton the experience of his amazing grace.

So the lesson. God reveals himself to us as he will, and most often the experience comes to a climax in some specific event or circumstance which otherwise would be accounted extremely ordinary.

(b) Secondly this story of Moses at the burning bush exposes *the mystery* of God's name. I put it like this, because when God revealed to Moses that he was to be God's instrument for freeing the Hebrews from the slavery of Egypt and Moses resisted, throwing back the question, 'But if they ask me what his name is, what am I to tell them?', God gave this enigmatic reply—'I AM who I AM. This is what you must say to the sons of Israel. I AM has sent me to you.'

I AM is God's strange name. We need not be surprised that down the centuries barrels of ink have been employed in writing down expositions of what the words may mean. All the famous theologians have attempted the task—Augustine, Aquinas, Luther, Calvin, to list a few. Most of them

14

have attempted philosophical explanations as if the name meant 'the ground of our being'. But of what reassurance could such an answer be for Moses in the situation in which he found himself—overwhelmed by the immensity of the task being laid upon him—the leadership of a whole people from the grasp of Egypt's mighty Pharaoh? What Moses needed was the reassurance that if God laid this burden upon him God would not desert him, would not leave him to carry it all himself, but would in fact go with him, support him, equip him and empower him. And this is what God promised. The name was his answer to Moses' resistance. 'I am with you. I am with you in all the circumstances, difficulties, demands and challenges you will have to face.' The name is in fact the assurance of God's presence with his servant—and with his servants throughout all the vicissitudes of life.

Is God's name vague? Certainly it is vague, but it is impossible for the human mind to grasp all that Godhead implies. None of us is able to comprehend more of God than is appropriate at our particular and individual stage of experience. The vagueness then is deliberate. God will make his presence known to us according to the circumstances of our needs *as they arise.*

In that well-written book by Alan Burgess called *The Small Woman* (Pan Books, 1959, 17th Printing, 1981), there is a captivating account of how that extraordinary London parlour-maid determined to go as a missionary to China, although no missionary society would sponsor her. She saved up sufficient money in 1930 to make the journey by the Trans-Siberian Railway quite alone. Arriving in Vladivostok, a completely unknown woman tapped on the door of the hotel where she was spending the night, warning her that if she did not escape at once she would never leave Russia. She said she would call for her within a matter of hours. She did so. There was a light tap on the door and there stood the woman. She only said, 'Follow me.' Gladys Aylwood, not knowing if this might be a trap, nevertheless followed. Down the stairs, through the entrance hall, out into the street, along the street. Never a word spoken. At length, this single file of two reached the docks where the stranger ushered Gladys into a shed, telling the man inside, a ship's captain, to take her to Japan. Then she vanished. Who was she? Why did she undertake this mission? The answers to these questions will never be known. But is it surprising that, if Gladys Aylward had not learnt it before, she certainly learned the lesson then, that God is the one whose presence is with us whatever the situation, meeting the need of the hour. In view of what was to befall her in China, she certainly had need of such a reassurance.

What is God's name? It is he who will be what we need when we need it. The Hebrews called him 'Yahweh' or, to use the traditional form in English, 'Jehovah', most often translated as 'The Lord.'

(c) Thirdly, the story of Moses at the burning bush tells us that the revelation of God which is given us in various places and in various times, mostly surprising, does not come primarily to increase our knowledge, but to encourage us *to commit our lives*, our persons, our enterprises and our futures into his hands where they are safe, and not only safe, but able to be fulfilled. Four times over in this account of the burning bush and its sequel, Moses resisted the call of God to the task required of him. In only one particular did God give way and that was to allow his brother Aaron to assist him. Otherwise the call to this service was insistent, and to inspire him for it, God showed him something of himself.

All significant work in God's service begins with a fresh vision of God himself, and all continuance of the same is with a consciousness never blurred of the fact of God's presence at hand.

So we return where we began. What is God's name? This, however, is not the fundamental question. The fundamental question is, what is God's name *for us*? What do we call God? What do we call God as the result of our experience? Creator? Judge? Redeemer? Father? They are all appropriate names. But for the Christian there is one name that makes them all come true,

'Jesus is the name we treasure,
Name all other names above.'

If then 'they ask me what is God's name', I shall know what
I as a Christian shall have to tell them—it is Jesus Christ our
Lord.

4. Law and Love

Exodus 19. 8(NEB) *The people all answered together, 'Whatever the Lord has said we will do.'*

There must be many who have had their attention drawn in
the last twenty years to a story something like the
following.

Here is a young woman in a prison camp in Eastern
Europe. There is no hope of her being set free except on one
condition—that she becomes pregnant. Pregnant women
were a nuisance in the prison and the easiest course for the
authorities was to discharge them. But how to become
pregnant? There is, however, one male guard who in spite
of the harsh conditions under which he is forced to work, has
retained some genuine elements of humanity. Out of concern
for the woman, and not for himself, he co-operated. She
becomes pregnant. She is set free. She has a husband who
will receive the child.

1 Situational ethics

And now the question. Is the prison guard guilty of immoral
action? That young woman will certainly be broken under
the harsh conditions of the prison work put upon her, and
in all probability die. If she can escape, there are chances in
her case of a new life. She has a husband waiting. Is the
prison guard wrong to make this new life possible? He does
not act out of selfishness. He wants to save the woman's life

17

and her future home. On the face of it of course, their cohabitation is immoral, but do not the circumstances justify it? Do they not make it moral?

And now a far more sweeping question. Ought situations *invariably* to condition the judgements we make on the morality of actions? Are we able to assert that if an action is performed out of love, it is thereby always justified? The position I am setting out, introduced by a somewhat crude story, goes under the general title of *situational ethics*. It is not uncommon today.

2 Mistakes about law

Thoughts such as these raise the whole question of the place of law in religion. Ought there to be any laws? It is not a question that can be avoided in any consideration of the place of the Old Testament in the Christian Church. 'The Law was given through Moses', we read in the first chapter of St John's gospel, 'grace and truth came through Jesus Christ'. Does not this sound the death knell of all reliance on law any more? Did not St Paul write to the Christians in Rome, 'For Christ ends the law and brings righteousness for everyone who has faith'? What are we doing then spending our time with the nineteenth chapter of the book of Exodus in the Old Testament? It tells of Moses setting before the elders of the people all the commands which the Lord had laid upon him and how 'the people all answered together, "Whatever the Lord has said we will do."'

(a) I suggest that first of all we notice that the commandments are given to the children of Israel *as a whole*. And they accepted them as a whole. They said, 'Whatever the Lord has said we will do.' What in fact those commandments accomplished was to shape up a distinctive way of life on the part of the nation. To put the matter simply and bluntly, there were certain things the people did not do. So their way of life became their identification mark. What is more, if they disobeyed, if anyone disobeyed, and persisted in disobedience, belonging to the nation was forfeited. That is to say,

18

keeping the laws was the condition of retaining membership. Notice, it did not create membership. God created membership by bringing the Hebrew slaves out of Egypt. What obeying the commandments indicated and assured was *keeping* a place among the people of God.

A first mistake the fashionable situational ethics makes is to assess moral questions on an individual basis. It is wrong to begin with this man, this woman, acting in this particular way in this particular situation and from it go on to make generalizations, and in the end to assert that there are no moral absolutes. We have to begin with what constitutes the life-style of the people of God. We cannot therefore write off those commandments and retain the distinctiveness of this people. They belong together. There cannot be this people without those laws.

(b) A second mistake is to set law and love in opposition to one another. It was out of pure compassion that God brought the Hebrews out of the slavery of Egypt. There was no particular worthiness in them to justify the action. The exodus was the outcome of God's unmerited favour, that is, grace. Are we to suppose then that, when those same Hebrews were welded into a nation at Mount Sinai through the leadership of Moses, God was now replacing love with law? Was he not rather continuing his loving-kindness to the nation *by providing law*?

Is this too hard to accept? Let me provide an illustration. Some time ago I was obliged to make a journey by car. My destination was, of course, clear, but not the route. I, in fact, got lost. In spite of the directions given me I came to the point of not knowing where I was. In these circumstances at night it is not difficult to panic; and consulting the road map with a flash lamp does not help. For one thing you do not know in which direction you are facing. So there is nothing for it but to try and make your way back to the point from which you set out and to follow those directions originally given. What a relief when you recognize the pub on the corner of the road you are told to look out for, and the church on the top of the hill, and a bridge over the

Thames some miles further on. How grateful you are by now for the directions. How stupid even to think for one moment that he who had invited you to visit him, had turned over to act harshly because he had provided you with markers for the journey. Quite the reverse, the directions were part of the kindness.

So commandments given to the people of Israel at Sinai were part of the kindness of God towards his people. They were identification marks but they were also keys to the rewarding way of living now.

(c) But still someone wishes to argue that law necessarily involves the destruction of freedom. Come back however to that car journey. Was I free without those directions provided by my host? Was I free when I was drawn up to the kerb under a lamp-post peering at the street names and anxiously consulting the road map to try to ascertain my whereabouts? Was I not a prisoner in the unknown, and a prisoner in my anxiety as to whether or not I should ever reach my destination or even the way back home? Was I not rather a free man as soon as I found myself on a road recognizing the markers that had been given me? Did not my spirits rise as soon as I was confident I was on the right road?

No, law does not necessarily mean the loss of freedom; it means the creation of circumstances in which freedom is possible. Freedom limited to a certain degree, no doubt, but then absolute freedom is an impossibility. If all the flowers in the garden have absolute freedom with no restrictions there will soon be a scarcity of flowers, for the plants will have choked each other.

Law then does not necessarily contradict love.

3   Christ and the law

Finally I return to a question already raised. Has the New Testament abolished the laws of the Old Testament? Does the Sermon on the Mount preached by Jesus, in which he stressed the inner motive rather than the external observance of moral laws, do away with the giving of the commandments on Mount Sinai? Some of his hearers may have wondered. Quickly however he settled the doubt. He said, 'Do not suppose that I have come to abolish the Law and the prophets; I did not come to abolish, but to complete.' What the Sermon on the Mount does is to set a higher standard than the law-giving on Mount Sinai. For one thing, the ten commandments are negative, 'Thou shalt not', whereas the teaching of Jesus is positive. A higher standard, yes, so high in fact that it is impossible of attainment by us—but the good news of Christ is that he reached it for us. He is our saviour, our saviour from our own despair at how often we fall.

But the commandments still stand. They stand for the old Israel, they stand for the new Israel, the Church; they are the standard by which our loyalty to Christ is measured. Christians like the elders at Sinai are bound to reply, 'Whatever the Lord has said we will do.' Christ implied as much when, according to the fourth gospel, he said, 'If you love me, keep my commandments.'

Maybe there are times when we fail. Maybe there are situations in which the strict keeping of the commandments is not to be observed. Maybe there are extenuating circumstances, but the decision as to what is right and wrong cannot be left to the intuition of the individual at the time when a choice has to be made, for his knowledge is limited and his heart fickle.

Every one of us needs to be guided by that for which the Church stands. It must stand for something. It must stand by that which has been given to it as a body. It must exhibit a distinct life-style in consequence. It must answer with the elders of old, 'Whatever the Lord has said we will do.' We are saved by belonging. And we show we belong by the extent to which we obey.

5. Judgement, Mercy and Forgiveness

Exodus 32. 14 (NEB) *So the Lord relented, and
spared his people the evil with which he had
threatened them.*

We do not like this text. It is the kind of text that turns us
off the Old Testament. We do not like the picture of God it
suggests. We do not expect God to have to relent about
anything, least of all about evils with which he himself has
threatened his own people. The text could conjure up a
picture of a father 'seeing red' because his son has disgraced
him by getting mixed up in an international drug racket,
telling him to get out and never to show his face in the home
again. And as for thinking he can expect financial as-
sistance—he can rub that idea out of his head! Late that
night, however, his wife 'talks him round' and he relents. He
spares his son the evil with which he had threatened him.
  What do you think of that father? Ought he to 'see red'?
Ought any of us ever to 'see red'?

1 Judgement

The first point this text establishes—unless of course we are
prepared to rub out the incident altogether, if not the entire
Old Testament—is that we really do have to deal with a God
who can become angry. I know that the late Professor
C.H.Dodd made the point that with God anger is an
impersonal force, an effect of man's rejection of God and not
an emotion, but our text is anything but impersonal. Here
God is angry and here he relents.
  And the New Testament is not silent about God's anger.
St Paul built his argument in the letter to the Romans on the
wrath of God. And if we assert that this is merely St Paul's
individually stern approach, we have to reckon with the

anger of Jesus in the gospels; anger with obstinate stupidity, hypocrisies and callousness. And was he not angry when he drove the traders out of the temple precincts, even tipping up their counters?

I want to ask if 'seeing red' is *necessarily* an evil reaction. (It can be of course if it gets out of hand, but so can almost any emotion). Take an example. Here is a terrace of what are sometimes called working-class houses where the walls are thin. The occupants of one house are suspicious about the screams they hear issuing from the unmarried couple's house next door, the screams of tiny children. They suspect baby-bashing. They have noticed the bruises on the childrens' arms and legs when they have played in the street. One however is quite undisturbed, he continues to puff his pipe and read the sporting news. He hears the agonized cries, but he does not stir. Another neighbour 'sees red' and marches off to rap on the door, and because there is no answer telephones the police. Need I ask who is the better neighbour? Who in fact is the better person? Need I go on then to press my point that God would not be a good God if there was nothing that excited his anger, slow though it might be in coming? He would be a callous—I was going to say *inhuman* monster—but it would have to be *undivine* monster.

We have to do then with a God capable of anger and if we refuse the idea we are left with a sentimental religion, deprived of judgement, which, far from strengthening, is in fact grossly debilitating. We should be better off without it.

2 Mercy

But what makes God pass judgement? What makes God angry? It is time now to turn to the passage of scripture from which my text was taken—'So the Lord relented, and spared his people the evil with which he had threatened them.' The reference is to what is commonly known as the sin of the golden calf. The Hebrew people, making the laborious journey across seemingly endless deserts to the new country promised them (but which never seemed to appear), became bored. Moses, their dynamic leader, was absent. And with his absence the faith which had turned a rabble into a purposeful nation faded till it too was absent. Then the worst happened. They substituted a metal god for the real God, a god they could see, a god that would make no demands, a god that would never grow angry at anything they did, or anyone else did. Indeed, a god they had made themselves, a brightly burnished golden bull-calf, an idol made with hands.

We ought not to miss the lame part Aaron, the deputy leader, played in all this. Was there ever any more futile explanation than that which Aaron gave? The people gave me their gold. I threw it in the fire and out came this bull-calf. What nonsense! But there is a subtle point here. When a people's traditional faith dies on them, that is, the faith which has largely made the nation what it is, a consultation is not arranged to decide what other gods to substitute; the discovery is made that other things have somehow or other *already* taken the place of the real God, almost automatically. One could be a political or economic theory, reckoned as the nation's real saviour; another, some scientific or technological expertise, or even the general concept of democracy or equality. Given these, all will be well. So it is believed. Or in the words of this Old Testament scripture, 'These are your gods, O Israel, that brought you up from Egypt.'

What happens then? God is angry. Angry because his sovereignty has been supplanted? Yes, but angry because the supplanting of the real God's sovereignty means in the long run the gradual decline of the nation's standards, efficiency and peace. God is angry *on behalf of his people.* It is precisely the kind of anger we saw exhibited by Jesus, anger with whatever was responsible for hindering people from achieving the high calling of which they were capable. I call this *compassionate* anger, anger in which there is a basis of mercy. So judgement is there in the heart of God, but compassion is there too.

3 Forgiveness

God is angry but God relents. This is the great proclamation of this scripture. God is not inflexible. God is not without mercy. God is ready to hear the cry of all who turn to him. What is more, God is ready to hear the cry of *sinners* who turn to him. What is even more still, God is ready to hear the cry of such as turn to him in intercession *on behalf of others.* Where in all the scriptures up to this point in Exodus is there such penetration into the character of God as in this drama of the sin of the golden calf and its sequel? And is there anything more important that we should know than what God is really like? For it is with him ultimately that we all have to do.

God relents. He relents in this story of the golden calf, showing that he is a God both of judgement and of mercy. If he were only a God of judgement he would be a tyrant. If he were only a God of mercy, there would be no standards, anything 'would go'. But he is a God of both judgement *and* mercy. It is a dominant theme of the Old Testament. Typically therefore Psalm 101, verse 1, reads, 'My song shall be of mercy and judgement: unto thee, O Lord, will I sing.'

Mercy and judgement, however, is not an easy combination. It is in fact a costly combination. Yes, even for God, especially for God. This is what the word 'relent' implies. It implies a battle to achieve it.

All this points forward to the great principle of forgiveness. No one who has not grasped this can be said to have grasped the central message of the Bible. This is why this story of the sin of the golden calf and its sequel is important. Forgiveness costs. It costs terribly. It costs because mercy and judgement battle together *in the act of forgiveness.*

In Corrie ten Boom's book *The Hiding Place* (Hodder and Stoughton 1972), there is a gripping passage about the cost

25

of forgiveness. To appreciate this, it is necessary to know the depths of humiliation through which this Dutch woman and thousands of other women were dragged in the horrible concentration camp for women at Ravensbruck run by the Nazis during the last war. Corrie was a devout member of the Dutch Reformed Church whose crime was hiding Jews in Holland from the murderous clutches of the Gestapo. Unmarried and aged fifty-one, not only was she, with others, all but starved to death, but, pot-bellied and spindly-legged through hunger as they were, they had to file past young Nazi guards stark naked for frequent farcical medical inspections and visits to the wash-houses. Corrie only survived the shame by remembering that Jesus was similarly degraded (for you can be sure that in the real thing he was allowed no loin cloth on the cross). Then it happened. Assisting in Germany after the war with the rehabilitation of civilian life Corrie attended a Church service in Munich where she had given a short address. Afterwards a man approached her beaming and bowing, thanking her for her message and adding, 'To think that, as you say, he has washed my sins away!' And he stretched out his hand to shake. Then she recognized him. He was one of the jailors in Ravensbruck who had stood at the wash-house door jeering and mocking the wretched women stark naked and shivering in a long queue, some having to be held up by others, so debilitated had they become. Said Corrie ten Boom, 'I tried to smile, I struggled to raise my hand. I could not. I felt nothing, not the slightest spark of warmth or charity. And so again I breathed a silent prayer. "Jesus, I cannot forgive him. Give me your forgiveness." As I took his hand the most incredible thing happened ... into my heart sprang a love for this stranger that almost overwhelmed me.'

Forgiveness is costly because in it mercy has to do battle with justice, but if mercy wins and forgiveness is offered, it is achieved through the grace of God, because that is what God is like.

So the cross of Christ remains for ever as the historical

witness that in the heart of God judgement on sin still stands, but mercy also stands *and triumphs.* So we have our gospel of God's forgiveness of our sins foreshadowed even if crudely by our text from the Old Testament. 'So the Lord relented, and spared his people the evil with which he had threatened them.'

6. God's Provision

Numbers 11.23 (NEB) *Is there a limit to the power of the Lord?*

It was in May 1944 that the American 442nd Regimental Combat Team landed in Naples. One of their number was ordered to set up a kitchen and supply tent. In doing so he observed twelve Italians, men and women, lurking in the trees, watching with fearful eyes. Then one called out, '*Signore*, we clean—kitchen, clothes, anything you want.' '*Quante lire?*' shouted the American. 'No, no *lire*', came the reply. 'Is nothing to buy. You give us garbage.' Thinking the Italians might be farmers wanting garbage for fertiliser, he said, 'Sure, go ahead; help yourself.' Whereupon the Italians surged forward to the tins, cramming the slop into their mouths, potato peelings, congealed stew, coffee grounds. The American stood aghast. He had seen his fellow GIs stub out cigarette butts in their mess kits, and others spit in the cans. 'Stop', he cried, 'You can't do that. You can't eat...' 'You promised', wailed the hollow-eyed Italian. 'We work...' The American turned away, all but sick. So this was what war was like. He had not seen hunger before. (From *True Stories of World War II*, Reader's Digest, 1981)

1 Sensitive to God's provision

I was reading a few days ago a commentary by a German

27

theologian, Claus Westermann, on the book of Numbers in the Old Testament, from which my text is taken. Chapters ten to thirty-six tell of the wanderings of the Israelites in the desert after they had escaped from Egypt, and before they settled in the land of Canaan. Over and over again three stark words stand out—hunger, thirst and weariness. Claus Westermann confessed that he had never grasped the terror of those words until he read those chapters suffering privations as a prisoner of war. There are situations where a dry crust of bread is accepted as a gift from heaven. The truth is, as Westermann says, the man who has no knowledge of God's saving preservation does not really know God.

John Austin Baker, Bishop of Salisbury, in his book *The Whole Family of God*, writes, 'Just once in my life, that not for long, I had to go without food because I had no money. It was a piffling hardship not worth talking about, but it gave me a glimpse I have never forgotten of what it might be like to be in that position again and again with no prospect of rescue such as I had.'

I too have had a 'piffling' experience. Mine was not to know, after I had embarked on my college course, from where on earth a large proportion of the fees were to come, although I had won a scholarship. My father was dead. The Church did not sponsor ordination candidates in those days... During the years that have followed I have seen Church life from a number of different angles—pastoral, theological, central administration. I wonder if God has ever been more real to me than in those early years when I kept a post card propped up in a place where I could see it every day on which I had written:

> Through each perplexing path of life
> Our wandering footsteps guide;
> Give us each day our daily bread,
> And raiment fit provide.

(P. Doddridge)

Perhaps my 'piffling' experience leaves ajar for me a door by which even I am able to be sensitive to Moses' words to the Israelites when they were hungry, thirsty and dead-beat with weariness, doubting if any relief was possible in such a wilderness—'Is there a limit to the power of the Lord?'

2   Gratitude for God's provision

God provides for us normally with sunshine, showers, seeds to sow and harvests to reap, but sometimes he lets us be led into the wilderness, lest we take these basic blessings for granted and fail to recognize that in the last resort he is the giver of all. So he provides *in the wilderness.* What he provides there is not lavish, nor is it luxurious, but it is enough, just enough, so that there is squeezed out of us gratitude for the small blessings of life; not that God is jealous for gratitude, but because life without gratitude is sour.

In one of James Herriot's books, (*The Lord God Made Them All* (Michael Joseph, 1981)) there is a story about this veterinary surgeon being called out one Sunday night to a couple ten miles away to look at their dog. The woman asked him into a shabbily furnished room one end of which was partly curtained off. She drew back the curtain and introduced her husband, Ron, in bed, a skeleton-thin man with hollowed out eyes in a yellow face. 'That's the patient', she said, pointing to a dachshund sitting by the bed. 'He's gone funny on his legs, he can't walk.' The 'vet' was struggling all this time with irritation for being called out on a Sunday for a case which could easily have waited a day or two or been brought to his surgery. Then Ron said, 'I were a miner. Roof fell in on me. I got a broken back. Doctor says I'll never walk no more.' And then after a pause and in a husky voice, 'I count my blessings. Ah suffer very little and I've got the best wife in the world.' The vet couldn't help wondering what his blessings were—the wife, obviously, the dog, which provided companionship when the wife was out, and the marvellous view across the Yorkshire Dales where he used to tramp for miles. That was all. By then the vet's irritation had seeped away. Driving the ten miles back home across the Dales he felt very humble . . .

Am I addressing someone who has forgotten to be thankful for the ordinary blessings of life we so easily take for granted? It is to be wondered if our whole nation with its passionate urge to preserve what are called 'living standards', hasn't got things out of proportion. Sometimes we have to learn some elementary lessons the hard way, and one of them is that in the last resort, even in times of normality and plenty, we are dependent on God, not only for the good things of life, but for life itself.

I suspect that God led the Israelites through the wilderness for some such reason as this. They needed the hurting experience of hunger, thirst and weariness so that they might be able to hear the answer to the question, Is there a limit to the power of the Lord? They knew it when God provided manna in the wilderness, water out of the rock, resting places by the way, and even a means of healing when they were bitten by serpents.

'Is there a limit to the power of the Lord?' Who cares when the going is good? But what when it is not so good? Sometimes the roughness is of our own making. Sometimes it is caused by circumstances over which we have no control, but have to stand by idly watching; a marriage, for instance, breaking up before our eyes, or a son mixing with the wrong company. Then Moses' rhetorical question is a live one, 'Is there a limit to the power of the Lord?' And even more, his implied answer—no, there is not. We would like to believe that God can provide, even in the wilderness.

3 Believing in God's provision

There was one incident in these wilderness wanderings of the Israelites which is of special significance. It was the time when the people suffered terribly from being bitten by snakes. (Thousands of people still die from this every year in India). It is not difficult to appreciate the terror of those Hebrews. To meet this desperate situation, Moses acted strangely. He fashioned a serpent of bronze, fixed it to a pole which he then erected for all to see, *if they would*. They were informed that those who looked would be cured, their snake bites would not be fatal. God would provide healing.

Did anyone put the question then—is there a limit to the power of the Lord?—It is a divisive question. We are led to conclude that some answered no, there is no limit to the power of the Lord. They looked and were healed. Others however said, yes, there is a limit. God can do nothing for us in this condition. And as for the bronze serpent, take it away! And they buried their faces in their hands, tossing in agony.

What does all this mean? Surely that God does provide for his people even in the wilderness and harsh patches of our lives; but to gain from all that he provides, it is necessary to believe.

This is an incident the New Testament takes up in one of its most famous passages—St John's gospel, chapter three. I will quote from the old version. 'As Moses lifted up the serpent in the wilderness, even so must the Son of man be lifted up: that whosoever believeth in him should not perish, but have eternal life.'

Is there a limit to the power of the Lord? Apparently there is, but the limit is not on God's side, it is on our side. God offers us his gifts, but he does not force our hand open to receive them. Such is the terrible reality of human free will that God, who has implanted it, will not infringe it. And if he did, we should not be responsible human beings any more but manipulated puppets on a string.

All this applies to the greatest gift of all that God has provided in the wilderness of our human folly, wilfulness and failure—Christ lifted up on the cross for the world to see. The extraordinary fact is the power of the Lord in this to heal. It has been so widespread, so operative, even in what

31

appeared hopeless situations of human degradation as well as in cultured circles, that the question might be asked, is there no limit? But there is—it exists on man's side. Some will not believe. For those who do, however, the promise set out in the fourth gospel, as elsewhere in the New Testament, is firm—'that whosoever believeth in him should not perish, but have eternal life.' Note the words, 'in him', implying confidence in a person and not assent to a theology. Here then is God's provision—eternal life through Christ crucified and risen—a provision so great, so available, who would wish to set a limit?

7.   When the Fantastic is Necessary

Numbers 22.28 (NEB) *The Lord then made the ass speak.*

I doubt if many people know the story of Balak, son of Zippor and Balaam son of Beor, and if they do I doubt if they will take seriously the cursing Balak required of Balaam or do more than write off as fantastic the piece about Balaam's ass talking, too fantastic to merit the attention of intelligent people. So first of all I need to retell the story.

1   The story

Balak was king of the territory east of the Jordan river, opposite Jericho called Moab, a rugged mountainous landscape. The day came when, to his utter dismay, looking down from a vantage point in the hills, he spied the plain, which flanked the river, filling up day after day with an alien people—Israelites. There seemed no end to them swarming into his territory. So numerous in fact were they that the possibility of his driving them out by armed force was remote, unless someone could lay a curse on them. And that he took seriously for he knew what most ancients knew (and some moderns), *and feared*, that humans do exist who possess the power of the curse, and it can be devastating. Then with relief he remembered Balaam, son of Beor. It would be worth the journey to Pethor by the river Euphrates to fetch him because what Balaam agreed to bless *was blessed*, and what Balaam agreed to curse *was cursed.* So a deputation was soon on its way to Pethor with ready money in their pockets, and this word on their lips from Balak— 'Look, a people newly come out of Egypt is covering the face of the country. Come at once and denounce them for me; then I may be able to fight them and drive them away.'

Forthwith the tussle began inside Balaam's conscience. He received the deputation, he saw the money bags and he listened to Balak's case. But, and this is why Balaam's story does not run smoothly, he also heard God's voice speaking to him. 'You are not to go with them or curse the people, because they are to be blessed.' So the deputation found itself on the road again back to Balak, back without Balaam, and without his curse.

Balak, however, was not a king to take no for an answer. A more powerful deputation was despatched to Pethor composed of more influential members, carrying heavier money bags and with this open-ended offer. 'I will do whatever you ask me. But you must come and denounce this people for me.' But still Balaam refused. 'Even if Balak were to give me all the silver and gold in his house, I could not disobey the command of the Lord my God...' But he did go. He went with the Moabite chiefs.

Then when Balaam in the company of two servants was riding his ass, the Lord was angry with him and caused his angel to bar his road, not once but twice, and no beatings of the poor beast by Balaam would make her go forward for she saw ahead of her what Balaam did not see. *So the Lord made the ass to speak,* and then Balaam's eyes were opened and he too saw the angel barring his road. And not only did he see, he also heard God's reprimand and order to go to Balak but only to utter the words he, God, would put in his mouth.

33

2   The lesson of the fantastic

The Lord then made the ass to speak—Numbers 22.28—this is the nub of this story. This is where its message lies. When God's servants fail to heed his word through ordinary channels he sometimes has to employ extraordinary means to open their eyes to what is right.

Here is a story. It is about a married couple who were constantly quarrelling. To do them justice they tried to hold back their arguments till after the children had gone to bed. But a little six year old heard. And one day when a slight divergence of opinion arose between the parents, the child unexpectedly spoke. 'Mummy, why are you two always quarrelling?' So the truth was out.

Sometimes a child lays bare what adults fail to recognize. And God, in his concern for his people, is sometimes driven to employ unexpected agents to bring them to face a truth they are unwilling to see.

There was that occasion in the life of Jesus when the chief priests and doctors of the law were refusing to recognize the unique spiritual leadership which was being enacted before their eyes. So God used urchins to cry out the truth— 'Hosanna to the Son of David.' The sophisticated adults protested, 'Do you not hear what they are saying?' 'I do', replied Jesus, 'Have you never read the text, "Thou hast made children and babes at the breast cry aloud thy praises."'

It may be a child, it may be the humblest, yet most faithful member of the congregation (or perhaps not so faithful), it may be an animal, the animal we 'take it out on', as we say, who speaks to us when we fail to hear the word of God by any other means. There are occasions when the fantastic is necessary. It may be God's warning when we have become blind and deaf to tne obvious; for if we will not pay attention to the ordinary, God will employ the extraordinary. It is a mark of his concern for us that this is so.

There are some extraordinary happenings in the world in the present. A fantastic growth of pentecostal religious groups; a fascination, not least among the young, with oriental religious cults; a hankering after the more authoritative forms of religious expression. To the traditional churches such movements seem 'way out'. Could they be God's voice of reprimand that we have lost the spiritual dimension to our religion in our preoccupation with administrative reoganization and liturgical reform?

Is this the message of Balaam's talking ass to our generation?

3 The lesson of the unexpected

And now this. No one expects an ass to speak. Numbers 22.28 may state quite plainly, 'The Lord made the ass to speak', but this scripture does not speak to us because no one *expects* an ass to speak. We dub it an asinine story. Expectancy, however, is the condition, not only of whether we hear anything from the lips of the apparently unpromising but whether the unpromising itself will be encouraged to speak.

A few days ago I was talking to a schoolmistress friend of mine, a classics graduate, who, having taught in what is called the 'private sector', has opted to teach in a large mixed comprehensive school. 'I have some hulking great boys in my class', she said, 'including about half a dozen skinheads. They supposed I would expect nothing of them, but when they discovered that I did, they gave up calling me by my Christian name (which I said they could if they wanted to), and reverted to Miss, and *contributed in the class.*'

We receive from the despised parts of life in proportion as we have an expectancy of them. This applies not only to class, race and a religion other than our own, but to the unexciting, unglamorous, dull and even repelling bits of life. We do not expect them to contribute anything of value and consequently they do not. The law of life is that we receive from people, places and experiences according to our expectations.

35

'The Lord made the ass to speak.' The ass is his and he made it. Which being so he can make it serve his purposes. The Lord is sovereign even over asses.

The sovereignty of God is what Balak had to learn. He thought that, given a man endued with the power of the curse, he could wipe out those Israelites, be they God's people or no. But the purposes of God cannot be overthrown. All this scripture is about the sovereign purposes of God. This is what the word 'almighty' means when applied to God. He can make all things serve his will. But we must understand that the will of God is gracious. To bless mankind, not to curse, that is his aim. Indeed, to bless Israel was what God wished Balaam to do. The gracious purposes of God will not however be reached if we rebel and take the path of our own choosing. Only in his will is our peace. And if we will not hear this truth through more ordinary channels, God may have to employ means as fantastic as those in the story of Balaam and the talking ass to bring it home.

8. What Leadership Requires

Joshua 1.6 (RV) *Be strong and of a good courage: for thou shalt cause this people to inherit the land which I sware unto their fathers to give them.*

Some years ago when I was the visiting preacher at a church in the West End of London, I was mildly rebuked by a member of the congregation for my sermon on Joshua. I had compared him somewhat unfavourably with Moses whom he succeeded as leader of the Israelites and who must be counted a veritable giant of a man measured by any standard. My objector said, 'You forget Joshua was a very great general.' The Rector told me afterwards that my complainant was himself a military man of some standing.

I deserved the rebuke. Joshua was the man for the task that lay ahead, the invasion of Canaan. Moses had chosen him, passing over his own two sons of whom we hear very little. Of this we can be certain. Moses appointed Joshua as his successor, laying his hand on him, because of the qualities he discerned in him; and these he had every chance of observing and testing, for no one lived and worked closer to Moses in his time of leadership than this man, Joshua. The proper question to ask about him is, What were the qualities of which he was capable, and which were demanded of him for the task of leadership that lay ahead for him? They are, I suggest, summed up in the words of God addressed to him at the outset of his campaign. 'Be strong and of a good courage: for thou shalt cause this people to inherit the land which I sware to their fathers to give them.' They tell us what leadership requires.

1 Strength

First leadership requires strength. A leader must be a strong man. Strength fascinates people. They will run after it, watch it and applaud it.

Strength here means physical strength; not of course brute force, for without intelligence behind it, futility will be the final word written across the energy exerted. Strength here means staying power, endurance, the capacity to go on and on, sometimes with few rest periods and very little sleep. People who have lived and worked close to those in high office never wholly get over their astonishment at the ability of their superiors to pass from a difficult interview to a difficult committee to a difficult official report to a difficult speech, blocking off the one from the other and laughing at some comic episode in between, day after day, burning the candle at both ends. Perhaps one of the most astonishing men of all time in this respect was Napoleon Bonaparte, who attended to affairs of State actually behind the field of battle which he was organizing.

This kind of strength is a pure gift. It is not always given to the strong at birth but develops in process of time. Albert Schweitzer is by no means the only example of a strong man who was puny as a child. Whenever it comes, this kind of strength is a gift and is one of the signs that the possessor of it may, not will—may be marked out for leadership.

We can take it for granted that Joshua possessed this kind of physical strength. As commander of the invasion forces of Israel it would be essential. But he must also have possessed that strength of mind which is more than cleverness but to which others will concede authority. Such a man scarcely needs authorization to exercise power, he has it in himself.

As we read the book of Joshua we sense the strength of this man. As a military commander he saw at once that Jericho, the rich but strongly fortified frontier town, was the gateway to Canaan. Jericho had to be taken first, and however we may interpret the strange story of the daily encirclement of the walls for seven days, we may at least deduce this—that he was the strong leader who knew how to hold back his strength till the moment was ripe for attack. What is more, he had strength sufficient to stop his troops from looting such prizes as the overthrow of the city brought within their grasp; and, when one did succumb to the temptation, to dispatch him forthwith. One is reminded of T.E. Lawrence's strong and lonely action in Arabia during the first world war.

'Be strong' were God's first words to Joshua as he was about to undertake the invasion of Canaan. Perhaps the command was scarcely necessary and Emerson got it right when he wrote, 'It is as easy for the strong man to be strong as it is for the weak man to be weak.'

2 Courage

'Be strong and of a good courage.' Strength physical, intellectual and moral is not the only necessity for leadership. There must also be courage.

Courage implies fighting. If we are unwilling for any kind of fight we have no need of any kind of courage. And the fighting is not necessarily aggressive. If a man is told he has a cancerous growth it requires courage to attend to business next morning as if no such diagnosis had been made. When we do wrong it requires courage to own up and 'face the music.' In such circumstances a fight is on. Courage and fighting, fighting and courage, go together. It was when a battle was imminent that Joshua was bidden to be courageous.

Courage also implies the running of risks. If we opt always for the safe seat we shall have little need to call on courage; but the prizes of life do not go to such.

I was reading the other day of how the civil rights movement was born in America and how Martin Luther King became its leader. It was born of courage. On 1st December 1955 a weary, hardworking woman named Rose Parks boarded a bus in Montgomery, Alabama, paid her fare and sat down behind the white section on the last empty seat. At the next stop six whites boarded the bus, but Rose refused to give up her seat to one of them as was customary. The bus driver ordered her to leave. Normally a quiet, good tempered, even shy woman, she refused. She was tired. She had paid her full fare. Then the bus driver grew abusive, stopped the bus, and had her arrested 'for violating the city's segregation ordinances.' She was put in gaol. As a result the black community appealed to a young and almost unknown Baptist pastor called Martin Luther King. With his wife he worked night and day over the weekend organizing a black boycott of all buses on the following Monday. They ran a terrible risk. The black workers had everything to lose if it failed. Anxiously the Luther Kings peered out of their windows. Would those buses really be empty? They were!

All day the buses were empty! The boycott was almost one hundred per cent effective. Courage to fight and face risks gave Martin Luther King the leadership of the civil rights movement. History was in fact made that day.

'Be strong and of a good courage.' Leadership is impossible without courage.

3 Faith

'Be strong and of a good courage: for thou shalt cause this people to inherit the land which I sware unto their fathers to give them.' As well as strength and courage, faith is necessary for leadership. For Joshua it was faith that God would make good his promises that his people would inherit the land.

If we do not believe in anybody or in anything we shall be weak people, and weak people accomplish very little. This surely is one of the dangers that confronts our whole country at this moment.

Joshua believed in the purposes of God for his people, and that he had been personally equipped and chosen to carry those purposes the next stage forward. Risk lay ahead. Roughness lay ahead. Setbacks would lie ahead, but a man who believes keeps going. 'This is the victory that over-cometh, even our faith', as the New Testament puts it.

Joshua, strong man though he was, courageous man though he was, and withal a competent military comman-der, would have made no mark on history without his faith. It is worth while noting in passing how many military men of the topmost rank in Britain's armies have been believing men. Their faith knits together their own gifts.

Conclusion

The book of Joshua is not a bare history of the invasion of Canaan by the Israelites. It is a heavily edited account to bring out the qualities of the man who led it. And, for us who are Christians, we cannot avoid noting that the name Joshua is an alternative for Jesus (see Hebrews 4.8 RV margin). He it is who leads us into the peace of God, what the Epistle to the Hebrews calls 'the rest of the people of God.' He was strong. Did not John the Baptist, his strong forerunner, cry—'There cometh after me he that is mightier' (stronger) 'than I.' And had he not courage to go steadfastly to his battle for the souls of men and women at his cross believing in the promises of God?

It is in the light of this leadership that the Church should exercise her leadership in the world, strong, courageous and believing. A weak Church will accomplish little, a Church choosing only the safe seats and avoiding risks will provide no inspiration for others to follow. A Church that has lost its faith is more than useless. There is a spiritual warfare requiring the Church's engagement. We cannot capitulate to the moral fashions of the times. But to win victories we shall need to listen to the words addressed to Joshua: 'Be strong and of a good courage: for thou shalt cause this people to inherit the land which I sware to their fathers to give them.' There is no leadership without strength, courage and faith.

9   Key Experiences

Joshua 24.14 (NEB) *Hold the Lord in awe then, and worship him in loyalty and truth.*

In his book, *The Clowns of God*, Morris West tells of a woman suddenly turning to ask her companion who had held high office in the Church—'What made you become a priest?' The question put him on the defensive. He had told only one person in his life. The details were not pleasant. As a Frenchman he had joined the *maquis* when war broke out. Baptised and confirmed, this was however, where his religion stopped. He was young, though with the *maquis*, a rifle, a pistol and a killing knife, he became a man overnight.

41

His special work was to haunt the hills and pick up secret messages of troop movements brought to him in an isolated shepherd's hut by a woman. She was about thirty, a farmer's wife whose husband had been posted missing. She was lonely. He was lonely. Basically they were both afraid. Then of course it happened. What would you expect? Neither saw any future ahead. And there wasn't for her. Some drunk Germans caught her, raped her, then pinned her to her own table with a kitchen knife. The young soldier found her thus. He did not forget. How could he? For years the memory goaded him. At last it brought him face to face with the brutality of the cross of Christ and the life and hope on the other side of it, his only life and hope, and the world's only life and hope he had come to believe. So he became a priest...

1 Key experiences

I do not know if the woman who drew this story from him by asking, what made you become a priest? had ever looked him up in *Who's Who* or *Crockford's Clerical Directory* (or whatever is the French equivalent). If she had, she would not have found this story nor even a reference to it. There would be his date of birth, his place of education, the year of his ordination, followed by a whole string of appointments, honours and probably publications; but not one word about his terrible encounter with love, brutality, a nagging conscience and at the last release before the crucifix. And yet nothing about the man's career was explicable without these experiences.

Nor is this only true of priests, but of generals, admirals, professors, engineers, business men, bankers, home-makers—who knows what secret events or train of events in the past have brought them to where they are and what they are? They are not the kind of experiences that can be recorded as history, anyway, because they are such subjective history, and being such, only make full sense to those who underwent them. To some outsiders (at least), they will be meaningless. Nevertheless the fact stubbornly stands. The subsequent life is inexplicable without these secret experiences lying in the background.

2 Foundation events in the Old Testament

I want to ask you to try and see the Old Testament in the light of all this. Perhaps you are frightened of the book. It is such a long book anyway, being a collection of books. And there are such harsh things in it, and some boring things, and quite a few passages which don't seem to add up to any kind of history as we know it in our twentieth century understanding. Take for instance the story of the children of Israel crossing the Red Sea, or the wilderness wanderings, or the giving of the ten commandments on tables of stone to Moses on the top of Mount Sinai. What are we to say of all this? It is not even possible to trace these places on a map! Old Testament scholars face these problems head on, and only attempt to set out what happened to Israel as a historical record (as we understand history today) from the settlement in Canaan, and not before. After the settlement we *can* confidently refer to maps, geographical features and the comings and goings of the surrounding tribes and nations. We can supply dates and get the leading characters of the various periods in a clear perspective. The books of the Kings in the Old Testament are like the entries in *Who's Who*. But—and this is the point to make again—the history of Israel is inexplicable without those half hidden events which preceded the settlement in the land of Canaan. Interpret them as you will, they refer to experiences of fundamental importance. They are in fact the key to the whole. 'What made you become a priest?' What made Israel become God's special people?

3 Four foundation experiences

At the risk of over-simplification I want to suggest that there are four foundation experiences in Israel's history which

43

contain all the elements from which the subsequent drama developed. They are the exodus from the slavery of Egypt, the giving of the law at Mount Sinai, the sin of the golden calf and the journey up to the promised land of Canaan. And in all this there is one dominating figure, a giant of a man by any standard, Moses. None of us will ever begin to understand Israel without these four foundation experiences in Israel's history, and the man who played the dominant role—Moses.

What happened at the Red Sea, sea of reeds or wherever was the place where that rabble of Hebrews escaped from the whips of their slave masters by the Nile? A press reporter would tell of freak weather conditions which gave these fugitives the chance of their lives to escape, and they took it. Moses, however, taught the people that God was their rescuer.

What happened at Mount Sinai? After the wanderings in the wilderness which made the refugees question the worth-whileness of their escape, they came to ask of Moses what was required of them in the way of conduct by their Deliverer, and he gave them the ten commandments. They were God's words, and in promising to obey them they were keeping a covenant with him.

What happened at the sin of the golden calf? The French artist Poussin has immortalized the scene for us in his great painting now in the National Gallery in London. The Hebrew people became bored with the laws which regulated their behaviour. In this they were not the last. And when they had turned their backs on the supreme God, they set up other gods of their own making. They were not the last in this either. We see it on a large scale in the twentieth century western world. But there, under Moses, Israel learned the meaning of forgiveness, the need of a mediator and the extraordinary grace and condescension of God. Never will the Old Testament be appreciated unless full attention is given to this basic experience in the wilderness of Sinai.

And then fourthly, after their arrested apostasy, led by

44

Moses the people approached the promised land. It is not possible, I think, for any in whose veins Hebrew blood does not run, to appreciate what the word land, *Eretz*, really signifies. On this very day when I am writing this sermon, the postman has brought me from the Tourist Agency in Israel a little tube (as if it were toothpaste), containing honey, and written round it the verse from Numbers, 'a land flowing with milk and honey.' Israel has not appeared like that to other nations, least of all to British troops serving there in the wars; but for the Hebrew people it is the land *God has given*. It is his gift to a small nation.

This is the point. In all four of these foundation experiences at the root of Israel's history *God* was believed to be at work, and in these experiences the character of God was made known.

4   *Loyalty to our own experience*

And now the initial text again. 'Hold the Lord in awe then, and worship him in loyalty and truth.' It belongs to the dated period of Israel's history. It constituted the appeal Joshua made to the nation at the time of its settlement in the land now entered and conquered. It said, in effect, be true to those early experiences of God in your life. It is there that your security rests. Never explain them away. Never doubt that it was God who called and God who led you. Never cease to worship him, for he is the Lord of all your life from the beginning to the end and even beyond the end . . .

Here surely is God's word to us in this scripture. Not everyone in the family of God's people has come there through the gateway of some startling conversion experience, probably only very few, and they may be reticent about what happened, so crude were the events at the time. But who is there of us who has not felt the hand of God at some time in his life—leading perhaps to a life's partner, or lifting us up from a bed of sickness, or deliverance as from some horrible pit, mental, moral or physical, into which we might so easily have fallen? The temptation is ever before us to

45

explain away these events as coincidences, or at least to rub out the remembrance of what we felt at the time to be the work of God; and then, worse still, to set up other gods whom we reckon are the real controllers of our destiny—the economic situation, the current state of medicine, the political climate of our day, or even our own will power. We should, however, hold in our minds those key events of the past in which God's presence was sensed, for they have brought us to the places where we stand. Hear then the text again, 'Hold the Lord in awe then, and worship him in loyalty and truth.'

10. Sparkling Deliverers

Judges 2.16 (RV) *And the Lord raised up judges, which saved them out of the hand of those that spoiled them.*

It is no use reading the book of Judges in the Old Testament if you are a staid old fuddy-duddy. The incidents it records are wild, daring, cheeky, boisterous and sometimes ridiculous, like Samson tying lighted firebrands to foxes' tails and letting them go among the Philistines' standing corn. You have to get into the mood of spirited youth to appreciate this book, perhaps even to remember some of the pranks you yourself 'got up to' when you were young. Volumes could be filled with the daft larks undergraduates have indulged in; and undergraduates are supposed to be above the average in intelligence and privilege! But youth is like that, and what needs to be remembered is that the book of Judges in the Old Testament records the youthful period in the life of the Hebrew people. It was chaotic, brilliant, idealistic and a bit bawdy all in one. But these were God's people, and like youth generally, the young people of that time laid hold of some important principles, even if they did (like youth generally), get them out of proportion.

1 Surprising leaders

First, we need to notice that the people who gave the lead in the early years of the Hebrew settlement in Canaan exhibited a strange medley of contrasting characters. There was left-handed Ehud, who made a double-edged dagger eighteen inches long and strapped it under his clothes on his right thigh. Visiting the fat king of Moab and kidding him that he had come with a secret message which he must deliver alone, he plunged the dagger into his belly and then escaped through the window... What a story to tell when he got back home!

And then that girl Deborah, who roused a whole army to attack the Canaanites marauding their land. And Gideon who knocked out the Midianite oppressors with a surprise assault by three hundred men tricking the enemy with lighted torches in jars. And Samson, whose tall stories about his forays into Philistia, his disastrous involvement with Delilah and his final desperate revenge on his captors at Gaza after he had been blinded, became legendary in Israel, and must have enlivened many a camp fire meeting.

What does all this 'rough stuff' in the book of Judges say? One thing, surely, with the utmost clarity. Never be surprised at the variety of characters God uses for his purposes. Not all of them will have 'short back and sides', twin sets or Oxbridge accents, though some will. Others will be shocking, rough, a trifle crude and very up-to-date. They will however all have one thing in common, they will have reacted powerfully, even if impulsively, to situations of crying need. They will feel called *to do something*. They will be people of action. They will be men and women of spirit.

Some of us have been called to live our lives in establishment circles. There is no need to be ashamed of this, no need to make excuses. God has his way for establishment types. But let us not make the mistake of being surprised when God raises up and makes use of people utterly different. The judges in the Old Testament book that bears this name, were not establishment judges of the kind we

47

recognise. They were God's sparkling leaders, and the sparkle they displayed was the work of the spirit. Indeed, it is of these men and their exploits that the Bible first uses the word spirit.

2   Unplanned exploits

Secondly, the deliverances from crises of need which these judges (so-called) effected were spontaneous reactions. They were unplanned. There had been no enquiry, no consultation, no committee decision, no recommendation, no official appointment of authorized officers, no 'white paper', no 'green paper'... What had happened was that the pressure of events on the whole community had caused one man, one woman, to be inspired to take action and to call all who would to join in.

Some of us have lived very close to planning. There is government planning and community planning. There is ecclesiastical planning and even evangelistic planning. We shall be most unwise to undervalue planning, but the book of Judges in the Old Testament warns us that it is also most unwise to *overvalue* planning. Planning can be a killer. It can kill off initiative, swiftness of action, spontaneity and sparkle like nothing else in the world.

There is another danger too about planning. It sets up structures, and those structures tend to stay in being after the need for their first formation has passed. Money even gets locked up in them. There must be millions of pounds of untouchable money in Britain at the moment, which could be used for present needs but cannot because it is tied to outworn needs. And *people* get locked in them. It gives them one-track minds and limits their adaptability and therefore usefulness.

The book of Judges performs this (perhaps unwelcome) service that it places a query against our General Synods, assemblies, conferences and local planning groups in our Church life. They have their part to play but if they interfere too strongly with spontaneity, the unexpected and the unusual, they hinder the work of God. Everything must not come under their control, nor must authenticity be accorded only to what they recognize. This is not to say the Spirit does not operate through committees, but it is to say that it very often operates apart from them altogether.

3 Loose ends

Thirdly, the book of Judges warns us against *following up* all our activities. We need to leave loose ends.

When these judges were called to knock out the Moabites, the Midianites, the Philistines, or whoever was the oppressor at the time, they rose up from their normal way of life, raised a following, did the job and then returned to their previous life as before.

All these activities were in the name of freedom. The deeds were done to be rid of oppression. And it is significant that it was the youth who felt called to give a lead in this campaign. So it is today. So it ever has been. Struggling for liberty is what fires the young. It is from this age group that revolutions are born, and subsequently are carried through. This however is the disappointing consequence of almost all revolutions in the name of freedom; a powerful group is set up to maintain the freedom of those that have been liberated and it becomes as oppressive as the original tyranny from which the struggle was made at considerable cost to be free. This is why revolutions are disenchanting.

Could it be that the book of Judges makes a strong point here? These sparkling leaders did not follow up their gains, they did not even establish their positions, they lived in the belief that should another crisis arise as it inevitably did, the spirit would enter another individual and cause him or her to carry out the exploits necessary to redeem the situation. They set up no institutional guarantees.

We find this a very hard word to hear. We rely on our institutions in the modern world all the way from the United Nations to the local parish council. We do not see how we can do without them, and maybe we are right; but this too

49

is right, that unless we also have inspirational leadership, leaders with *charisma*, we shall sink down into a dead level of mediocrity and feebleness, a likely prey for any clever foe that would wish to destroy us.

4 Encouragement and warning

So there are positive lessons to be learned from this wild book of Judges, and the young especially can be thankful that room is found in the Bible for bubbling, effervescent, even dangerous thrusting action. I do not forget the reminder J.B.Priestley gave us in 1940, that we owed the deliverance of our country from defeat by the German Luftwaffe to the young men who annoy us so much with their noisy motor cycles, for it was they who flew the Spitfires that did the job.

Nevertheless, we can get this indebtedness to youth, this spirit and dashing action out of proportion. We can get the book of Judges in the Old Testament out of proportion. Thank God it is there, but it is only one book. It does not constitute the whole Bible. Moreover, it represents only an interim period in the story of the Hebrew nation. There was the entry into Canaan and there was the subsequent establishment of the monarchy, and in between this patchy period of the Judges on which the book itself makes this comment in its final verse, 'In those days there was no king in Israel: every man did that which was right in his own eyes.' We do not usually read what some of them did as recorded in chapters 19–21 of the book, not in public anyway.

So the book gives us an encouragement and a warning. The encouragement is to give the young a chance, to give youthful spirits a chance, to allow plenty of room for inspiration, action and the taking of quick decisions in place of too much reliance on committees and planning. The warning however is not to disregard the necessity for law and order if a community is to be preserved from defeat through internal chaos. Perhaps all this has some special word for the

50

charismatic movement in Christian circles which is partly a characteristic of the present. We need the life this movement has brought but its benefits will be lost if we imagine we can have them without structures, even ecclesiastical structures. Does this smack of compromise, or watering down, so hated by the young? But does it not reflect wisdom? Remember this, the whole life of Jesus was lived under the inspiration of the Spirit, but he did not leave the ordered life of the synagogue, till its jealous leaders thrust him out. He held them both together.

11.   Freedom to Choose Wrongly

1 Samuel 8.7(NEB) *The Lord answered Samuel, 'Listen to the people and all that they are saying; they have not rejected you, it is I whom they have rejected, I whom they will not have to be their king.'*

I wonder if you have ever had the experience of being dropped? I mean metaphorically speaking. It could have been at school. You took it for granted that you would be playing with the first XI in the next football fixture; or in the tennis team against your chief rivals, but your name wasn't there on the notice board. You had been dropped. Am I overstating the case when I suggest that you felt sore inside, terribly sore? You took days to get over it.

But here is a bigger platform. A firm in the city of London where the head of one of the departments has worked for years seeing the business prosper under his administration. Fresh employees however were taken on, men who had undergone business training in America. They made it known to the management that in their opinion the organization was old fashioned. Changes in the departmental heads were required. And so this man who had given of his best and seen results, was dropped. The dismissal was

51

expressed nicely, but it was dismissal. He never got over it.

The first book of Samuel brings to our attention a case of being dropped. Samuel was a great man, almost a kind of Renaissance type, so all-round was he—prophet, priest, administrator, judge; and withal a spiritual quality Israel had not seen for decades, retained from his youth. Foes were kept at bay under his leadership, internal corruption kept in check. But the people wanted him dropped. True, his sons came nowhere near his standard, but their inferiority was not the real reason. People had been taking note of the superior efficiency of those surrounding nations that were governed by a king. It was a king they wanted, and Samuel dropped. The Biblical account is blunt. 'So all the elders of Israel met, and came to Samuel at Ramah and said to him, "You are now old and your sons do not follow in your footsteps; appoint us a king to govern us, like other nations."' Put yourself in his shoes. He was being dropped. And terribly sore, he fell on his knees in prayer to God. What better could he do?

1 God comforts

The first point for us to notice is that God comforted this sore man. Perhaps we can scarcely believe it, but God cares about people being dropped. He understands. He understands our feelings, and if he does not approve of our resentments, he does understand them. He even understands our cursings and our bitterness, wrong as they are in his sight—or why do they stand there written in the Psalms—terrible imprecations, offensive surely to all Christian ears.

God however took the sore upon himself. This is what this scripture says. 'Listen to the people and all that they are saying; they have not rejected you, it is I whom they have rejected, I whom they will not have to be their king.' Many decades were to pass before this divine assumption of our sorrows was to be spelled out, but it did happen. We can read it in Isaiah 53. 'Yet on himself he bore our sufferings, our

52

torments he endured...' Here then tucked away almost unnoticed in a dark, if not crude, early period of Israel's history, is this tiny pinpoint of light, barely lighting up this truth of God incarnate.

'In every pang that rends the heart,
The Man of Sorrows bears a part.
He sympathizes with our grief,
And to our suffering sends relief.'

And when our sorrows merge into sins, as they can so easily do, blocking out the sense of God's care and God's presence, so thick does the blanketing cloud of self-pity become, then God does more than bear them sympathetically, he actually bears them away. This is the experience of forgiveness which Christians lay hold of in the cross of Christ.

There is a story that has come out of the second world war of a Polish priest called Father Maximilian Kolbe. He was a prisoner in Auschwitz in July 1941 when the German commandant announced that ten Poles would be starved to death because of some infringement of camp rules. When the list of names was read out, one so named broke down and wept. He knew he would never see his wife and children again. But he did live to see them again, for from out of the serried ranks of prisoners there stepped forward Father Maximilian Kolbe who said quietly, 'I would like to take his place.' With the nine others he went and was starved to death. That was in Auschwitz in July 1941.

I hope I am enough of a theologian not to press this substitutionary aspect of Christ's sacrificial death too far, but somehow or other, God in Christ does not only comfort us but *covers* us in all our afflictions wherein we are afflicted.

2 *God lets us choose*

And now a second point. Expressed bluntly, the people wanted to be ruled by a king, whereas God wanted Israel to be a theocracy. That is to say, Israel wanted one thing, God wanted another thing. This was the problem. It is not a dated problem. On the contrary, it is a perennial problem. And not only in the experience of nations, but also in the experience of individuals.

Expressed bluntly also is the cost of what the people were asking: 'This will be the sort of king who will govern you,' said Samuel. 'He will take your sons and make them serve in his chariots and with his cavalry, and will make them run before his chariot. Some he will appoint officers over units of a thousand and units of fifty. Others will plough his fields and reap his harvest; others again will make weapons of war and equipment for mounted troops. He will take your daughters for perfumers, cooks, and confectioners, and will seize the best of your cornfields... He will take a tenth of your grain and your vintage to give to his eunuchs and lackeys. Your slaves, both men and women, and the best of your cattle and your asses he will seize and put to his own use. He will take a tenth of your flocks, and you yourselves will become his slaves...' We might put this in a nutshell by saying—the establishment of an absolute ruler will involve direction of labour, conscription and oppressive taxation.

Then there follows this: 'When that day comes, you will cry out against the king *whom you have chosen*; but it will be too late, the Lord will not answer you. The people refused to listen to Samuel; "No", they said, "we will have a king over us; then we shall be like other nations, with a king to govern us, to lead us out to war and fight our battles." So Samuel, when he had heard what the people said, told the Lord; and he answered, "Take them at their word and appoint them a king."'

I am aware of course that there are two accounts of the origin of the monarchy in the first book of Samuel, and this which I have outlined is the later one, coloured, no doubt, by later events. Do not however miss what the book is saying. When we set our own ways over against God's ways, he lets us have what we want. 'Take them at their word', he said to Samuel, 'and appoint them a king.' God forces no one into alignment with his will. The freedom of man, the independence of man, is something God will never repudiate. He will warn us of the consequences of our responsibility, but he will not cancel out that responsibility. Our lives are ours to do with as we will. If we choose secularism God will not interfere, or materialism, or the arms race, or Marxism, or capitalism, or racism, or pornography, or abortion on demand, or child battering—God will not reach down from heaven and put a block before our schemes. 'Take them at their word', says God in effect, 'and give them what they count to be superior ways of conducting their affairs . . .' This is the awful truth the first book of Samuel places before our eyes. We may not be free of anything else in life; our genes, our heredity, our environment, our social class, our background, our past sins and our present prejudices, they bind us like ropes we ourselves have partly woven, but, and this is the awful truth, we are entirely *free of God*, we can choose our own individual way and he will not intervene.

3 God acts graciously

One more point, also from this first book of Samuel—God will make the best he can out of the paths along which we freely choose to go.

Forgive, please, at this point, a word of personal admission (but a preacher lacks sincerity if he is not willing on occasions to show his hand). I have, more than once in my life, who hasn't?, come to the cross-roads when I could have turned right or left. I did not know which road to take. I prayed, but still I did not know, yet choose I must. Perhaps I took the wrong turn. All I can testify is that it was a source of strength to me to know that even if I had chosen wrongly God would make the best possible out of it—perhaps even better than if I had chosen the right road in the first place. This is the wonder.

So the books of Samuel in the Old Testament teach us. Israel chose a king. Their choice was not what God wanted but he did not intervene. And the king they chose turned out to be a failure. Saul the impressive warrior became morose and mad. Ah, but his successor was king David, a man whose consummate skill as a leader and genuine spirituality became for all Israel for ever the type of the ideal king, even the pattern of Messiah himself in whose lineage the Christ, when he came, did not scorn to see.

God gives us what we choose, and will not, if we are humble, damn us with the consequences; he will instead bring something better out of it than either we desire or deserve. Such is the grace of God.

I could leave you in the face of this scripture with a theological, perhaps even a philosophical, conundrum which all that this scripture says undoubtedly raises; the co-relationship of man's freedom and God's sovereignty. It is incapable, I think, of a rational solution. We must hold the two in tension. The practical lesson however is plain. God will make good flow even from our errors; nay more, even the errors themselves he will take upon himself. Such is God, and such is the glimpse of him that the story of Israel demanding a king, contrary to the divine will—offers. What a story! What a God!

12   Why Jerusalem Survives

2 Samuel 5. 6,7 (NEB) *The king and his men went to Jerusalem to attack the Jebusites, whose land it was. The Jebusites said to David, 'Never shall you come in here... None the less David did capture the stronghold of Zion, and it is now known as the City of David.'*

About the year 1000 BC a young man of distinguished appearance stood with a band of other dedicated soldiers gazing with intent eyes at a small fortress so impossible of access on three sides that it had for centuries withstood all attempts at capture. Perhaps Castle Rock in Edinburgh can give us a picture. The troops occupying the fortress derided the very idea of capture, shouting down with sneers and oaths to the soldiers in the ravine below that even blind men and lame men could defend their stronghold. But it was captured. How is not known for certain, but there is a suggestion that a small commando-like party daringly squeezed themselves up the water tunnel which led them into the very fortress itself. Swords and daggers did the rest in a matter of minutes. So King David took the place called Zion, the name for the promontory on which the fortress was built, later to be known as the city of David, and more generally as Jerusalem.

David wanted it badly. For seven years he had been king over the southern tribe of Judah at Hebron, but his aim was to be king over all the tribes of Israel and Judah, and for this he had his eye on Zion. Zion never had belonged to any Hebrew people. At the invasion under Joshua the Jebusites could not be dislodged, the Judges who followed could do nothing about it and King Saul left it alone. If therefore David could take Zion, none in any tribe could make a rival claim. Zion would be David's and David's alone. From its independent security he could exercise his authority with power over the whole land; which thing he did, and that with dazzling success. Events had a way of turning out well for David.

1   The painful city

You can't be a Christian and not take Jerusalem into your reckoning. As it happens you can't be a Jew either or a Muslim, for all these religions count it their holy city. This then is the fact, Jerusalem is the place where the encounter with God and man takes place; or to speak in more general terms, the place where ideals clash with realities. There is always a clash in Jerusalem. The place entered into the broadstream of history with the clash of David's sword and dagger with those of the Jebusites defending the fortress at

Zion. Swords, bullets and bombs have never ceased for long to resound among the buildings of Jerusalem which means 'city of peace', an unrecognizable title except ideally.

Sir George Adam Smith, in his remarkable two volumes on Jerusalem, published in 1907, has this to say about the city before even the first world war took place, let alone the events that have followed. 'Few cities have been so often or so cruelly besieged, so torn by faction, so sapped by treachery, so inflammable to riot, so drenched with blood . . . The bare catalogue of the disasters which have overtaken Jerusalem is enough to paralyse her topography. Besides the earthquakes which have periodically rocked her foundation, the city has endured nearly twenty sieges and assaults of the utmost severity, some involving a considerable, others a total, destruction of her walls and buildings; almost twenty more blockades or military occupations, with the wreck or dilapidation of provincial edifices; and frequent alteration of levels by the razing of rocky knolls and the filling of valleys; about eighteen reconstruction embellishments and large extensions, including the imposition of novel systems of architecture, streets, drains and aqueducts athwart the lines of the old.'

It is to be wondered how much, or if any of this terrible story has entered our minds as we have stood in Westminster Abbey, or some other place of Christian assembly to sing with fervour the lines of Parry's glorious setting, '. . . till we have built Jerusalem in England's green and pleasant land.' Who is to be blamed for asking the question—but do we want it? Should we not be better off without it? In truth it is here that the finger is put on the most sensitive point of human existence. This then is what Jerusalem in the first place stands for, even embodies, the unending struggle of human existence never far from pain.

2   The eternal city

If however Jerusalem means pain, it also means a future. Not the least remarkable fact about this place is that no one has ever been able to get rid of it—and it is not for want of trying. Sennacherib of Assyria made the first serious attempt in 701 BC, but fearing an attack on his armies in the rear abandoned his siege. You can read about it in 2 Kings, chapters 18 and 19. Then in 586 BC there came the first great destruction of Jerusalem and all that the kings of Judah had built up since David's day. This was carried out by the ruthless forces of Nebuchadnezzar, king of Babylon. Years later it was built again and years later destroyed again. Over and over this melancholy story of destruction and rebuilding repeated itself, but Jerusalem is still there. The Israeli Air Lines will fly you to see it, an impressive modern city grafted on to tiny remnants of the old.

Why has Jerusalem survived down the centuries? Certainly not because of that strategic position militarily which formed no small part of King David's attraction to the place. Nor because it is a source of mineral wealth; Jerusalem has nothing to offer in this respect. Even its water supply has to be pumped down from the Lake of Galilee. Nor because its surrounding land is abundantly fertile and productive of agricultural products, the desert in fact comes almost up to its gates on the east side. Nor because Jerusalem is outstanding as an architectural monument to the skill of man; there were even in the ancient world a number of cities far superior to Jerusalem in this respect. And it cannot be said to have produced a philosophy, art or music, to give it a name above other names. No, Jerusalem has survived because of something intangible and economically worthless—its religious associations, its testimony to faith in God, its belief that God actually makes himself known to ordinary men and women.

Jerusalem tells us simply by being there that religious faith is tough. Men may repudiate it, ridicule it, relegate it to the unimportant areas of life as a kind of optional extra, or even seek to stamp it out altogether as in Soviet Russia, but still it survives. Sometimes it only just survives. At other times it regathers extraordinary momentum. Religious faith is in fact very like the city of Jerusalem where David conceived the temple which Solomon actually built. Religious faith is tough, but why is it so tough? Is it because man is a religious animal? Is it because there is in man an inbuilt God reference? Is it not rather because religious faith points away from itself, away from the temporal, away from everything that is passing and transitory, it points to the place where eternity is grounded, the Being of God himself. Man is unable to destroy God. This is why faith which points to him cannot be rubbed out. It is also why Jerusalem, be it a fine city or a heap of stones, will always have a future and always be significant. Jerusalem is an eternal city.

3   The gospel city

And now I have to ask why was Jesus crucified there? Why was he not crucified in Rome or Athens, Antioch or Alexandria? You say, because he was a Jew of first century Palestine. But your answer is not big enough. If Jesus is the one through whom God pre-eminently speaks to man, and not simply to the Hebrews or Near Eastern peoples, why choose Jerusalem? What is it that is special about Jerusalem? Readers of the gospels in the New Testament will know that Jesus took good care that the hostility which was mounting up against him in his ministry did not erupt too soon so that he would be killed before he reached Jerusalem. It was there he chose to die. Why?

And we have to ask more searching questions still—If Jesus is God's word to man, why did he not ascend some authoritative seat, if not in Athens or Rome, then in Jerusalem to speak to the world? Why go to Jerusalem *to die*?

One answer I have already given—because Jerusalem is the place where the human conflict is most sorely experienced. Jerusalem is a city of pain and sorrow; not the flat, deadening pain which constitutes so much of the story of mankind, but the pain of longing, idealism and aspiration which issues in an interminable sequence of destruction and rebuilding, rebuilding and destruction. God comes to speak at the weary place of man's defeat of all that is best in him.

And the age-long defeat at Jerusalem sweeps over Christ too. He is defeated. He shares in Jerusalem's defeat. He identifies with man at the place of his supreme disappointment and frustration. So the Holy City (so called), the city of David, Zion, the centre of divine worship, becomes the city of blood. But from there God speaks in Christ. What is more, because Jerusalem is not only the city of pain but also the eternal city, it is at Jerusalem that he rises from the grave, promising and providing for men an eternal future. So Jerusalem becomes *the gospel city*. At the point of man's failure, which God in Christ shared, the resurrection took place.

You cannot be a Christian unless you take Jerusalem into your thinking. Jerusalem stands for man's most heartbreaking failure, but it also points to his eternal destiny. When those soldiers surrounding young king David stood gazing up at the fortress at Zion, they intended to capture, they accomplished more than they knew. Jerusalem entered into our human destiny. It entered supremely through him whom we know as the Son of David, Jesus Christ the Lord. We cannot be Christian and not take Jerusalem into our reckoning. It is there we hear the gospel of man's salvation.

13.   A Spoiled Prince

2 Samuel 19.4 (NEB) *The king hid his face and cried aloud, 'My Son Absalom; O Absalom, my son, my son.'*

There are six whole chapters devoted to Absalom in the Bible, and they cannot find one good word to say for him. Not that they revile him, castigate him or even pass judgement on him, they simply tell his story, and pretty sordid it is.

It begins with an account of rape. It is not long since the very mention of the word in any decent society, let alone the pulpit, would have been unthinkable; but scarcely a day passes now without some account of this beastly thing in the newspapers. So don't write off the Bible as concerned only with some unreal world of unnatural piety in which people do not move about as they actually are... 2 Samuel 13.14 reads, 'He would not listen, but overpowered her, dishonoured her and raped her.' This is not what Absalom did, but Amnon, another of King David's sons, he raped Absalom's sister, a beautiful girl called Tamar. It sparked off the trouble which ended in Absalom's death and King David's mourning—'The king hid his face and cried, aloud, "My son Absalom; O Absalom, my son, my son."'

1   An unsatisfactory home

If we are to let this story make its impact, we must begin with Absalom's home. It was most unsatisfactory. Of course it was privileged. Absalom was born into a royal household. There was money in plenty, and pleasure in plenty, and prospects in plenty—but for all that it was most unsatisfactory. It was riddled with jealousies because not one man and one woman ruled over it, but one man and a *number* of women in the form of polygamy. This was the fatal flaw. In a way King David is not to be blamed for this, polygamy was the way of the world a thousand years before Christ, and still is in Islam and many an African country; but because a practice is common, the cancelling out of the consequences does not follow. Polygamy breeds jealousy, and jealousy breeds hate, and hate, as often as not breaks out into violence. It did in the case of Absalom.

The trouble starts in the woman's heart, the unfortunate woman who has only half, or a quarter, or indeed, only a tenth, of her man's love. She craves of course for more, and when it is not forthcoming, as it cannot in the nature of the case be forthcoming, she lavishes all her pent-up affection on the child of that semblance of a marriage, spoiling the child, and being spoilt by the child who cannot give back the love she desperately needs.

So Absalom grew up in an atmosphere of unremitting tension, and not only tension but strife, active strife, because one woman would encourage her child to gain the ascendence over the child of another woman, subconsciously seeking to demonstrate the superiority of her union with the man they shared in common.

The Bible is unexpected in its method. It does not 'get at us'. It does not preach at us in the way most people think of preaching. It does not even castigate polygamy. It simply tells a few stories about what happens where there is not one man and one woman in a faithful marital relationship. It says, 'Look at the children. Look at what happens to the parents.' Such is the story of Absalom coming to grief and this lament, 'The king hid his face and cried aloud, "My son Absalom; O Absalom, my son, my son."'

2 A doting father

An unsatisfactory home background was not Absalom's only handicap for life, he also grew up with a doting father. Once again it is hard to blame King David. He was a warm man, quite unlike the oriental despots of his time, or of any time.

He was no tyrant in the home or anywhere else; he loved people and easily won their love in return, both men and women. Affection was part of his nature. And when this good-looking boy came on the scene, he could scarcely take his eyes off him. And when he grew to be a man, and as the biblical account puts it—'No one in all Israel was so greatly admired for his beauty as Absalom'—David's admiration swelled to doting.

Good looks can be a hindrance. They can lead to vanity and the word vanity means emptiness. Empty people run the risk of being unable to achieve any kind of stature as regards character and certainly of laying hold of life eternal. Parents who spoil their children actually place their souls in jeopardy. Good looks are a kind of wealth, not limited to those so stunning in appearance that they can make a fortune on the films. Jesus said, 'How hard it will be for the wealthy to enter the kingdom of God'—not impossible, note, but hard, indeed he went on to say, 'to God everything is *possible*.'

We talk much these days about the need for discipline among the young, but the prior discipline required is that of the parents. Parents need to discipline themselves not to give their children too much; too much money, too much pleasure, too much attention. The easier course is to give way, to give in, and to follow the fashion, and to do so out of sentiment, especially if the child is ill, weak or has some disability. How to combine wisdom with love does not come easily to any warm-hearted, generous person, let alone parent, but real kindness is the outcome of achieving it.

I read somewhere recently of a young man who had suffered a severe accident which would leave him for the rest of his life without the use of his hands. One day, lying in a hospital bed, he longed for a cigarette and called the nurse. She came, listened to his request and went away to fetch a whole packet which she placed on his chest. For an hour at least he struggled with that packet, endeavouring to tear the cellophane wrapping with his teeth and to get at the cigarettes. He achieved it. Then he called for matches. At

64

once she brought a box, placing them too on his chest, but departing at once to carry on with her duties. He never achieved striking the match or lighting the cigarette, but after some time the same nurse came to do it for him. 'If ever you are to make a success of your life when you leave this hospital,' she said, 'you'll have to learn how to do things for yourself—*somehow*.' I guess that girl would have loved to wait on that brave young man hand and foot, but *for his good*, she did not. I call that discipline of the highest order.

Of this mastery of sentiment, King David knew nothing, and the result was a spoilt child, a conceited man, a schemer, a rebel, a man of violence, and almost a destroyer of a whole kingdom. Overdrawn? No, not in the case of Absalom. Read the story for yourself in 2 Samuel, chapters 12–19. It will hold your attention to the bitter end. And remember this, the consequences of actions come in proportion to the size of the stage on which they have to be carried out.

3 An ambitious man

Absalom was an ambitious man. When anyone possesses gifts, man or woman—brain-power, skills, physical beauty—it is natural to want to capitalize on them. Nor is this wrong. Gifts are there for using, not for wasting. Ambition is not a sin. Everything does, however, depend on the methods the ambitious are prepared to employ, and the lengths they go to achieve their goals.

Absalom would stop at nothing, and not the least dangerous trait was his way, his patience; he was no hot-headed blunderer. Cool, calculating and scheming, he was prepared to wait for years to achieve his purposes, but when the moment for striking came he would strike hard. Blood on his hands did not worry him, nor the burning of his neighbour's field of barley to bring him to his heel. Even so, the king, knowing all this *and* all but toppled in his kingdom (for it was the throne of Israel that Absalom wanted), excused him to the disgust of his closest followers, so besotted was he on his favourite, spoiled and undisciplined son.

So at last we come to that fantastic, even macabre, scene of Absalom dangling from a tree, caught by his hair as he rode his mule beneath it in that last rebellious battle. Thus alone, helpless and desperate, the outraged commander of the king's army, sick of this young bragging traitor, seized his opportunity to thrust him through with well-aimed weapons. So Absalom's short and showy life came to its violent end—a pit in the forest for a grave and a great heap of stones raised upon it for a memorial. Ambition can bring a man to his ruin for all the undoubted gifts that he possesses, if he has been led to believe that he alone counts.

But is there no word of God for us in all this lurid tale? There is scarcely any mention of him in all its ins and outs. For Absalom God was not one to be reckoned with. Perhaps however we could hear this word. God is no almighty, doting Father. God does not spare the rod and spoil the child. God does not steer his children away from the troubles of life because they look to him, nor leave them out of sorrows because they put their trust in him. God is concerned for our temporal welfare, but also for our eternal destiny. Of all this the unknown author of the epistle to the Hebrews in the New Testament reminds us by his writing—'You have forgotten the text of Scripture which addresses you as sons and appeals to you in the words:

"My son, do not think lightly of the Lord's discipline, nor lose heart when he corrects you;
for the Lord disciplines those whom he loves;
he lays the rod on every son whom he acknowledges."'

66

14. Revolution

1 Kings 11.26 (RV) *And Jeroboam the son of Nebat,
an Ephraimite of Zeredah, a servant of Solomon,
whose mother's name was Zeruah, a widow woman,
he also lifted up his hand against the king.*

On the 9th April 1945 in the concentration camp at
Flossenburg, Pastor Dietrich Bonhöffer was hanged with
others including his brother-in-law, so paralysed as a result
of his tortures that he had to be carried on a stretcher into
the room. In one corner a movie camera operated, so that
the same evening in the Reich Chancellery Hitler was able
to see these men being hanged from hooks in the ceiling.
Even before the war Hitler counted Bonhöffer his enemy,
and when Bonhöffer was implicated in the preparations for
the plot which culminated in the attempt on Hitler's life on
July 20th 1944, he was thrown into prison. At one time this
German pastor had been a pacifist. It is not surprising
therefore that the question should be asked how he came to
be involved in a *coup d'état.* He himself had given his answer
to that question long before. If a pastor saw a madman
driving a car insanely down the road, crashing all life in the
way, he would not stand around merely to give absolution
to the victims before burying them, but would try to jump
on the car and wrench the wheel out of the madman's
hands.

I come back now to my text. 'And Jeroboam the son of
Nebat ... he also lifted up his hand against the king.' Was
he right to do this? Does the Bible approve of this action? Is
it ever right to rebel against the State? Is a *coup d'état* in any
circumstances justified? What are we to think about
revolutionaries? These are not irrelevant questions in our
modern world, so maybe the story of Jeroboam the son of
Nebat has something to say to us.

67

1 An Old Testament rebel

Let us look first at his history. Jeroboam came up the hard way. His mother was a widow which meant in those times pitiful poverty. It also meant that Jeroboam began in obscurity, than which there could be none greater than belonging to the vast labour gang drawn from all over Palestine to work on Solomon's building programme on Mount Moriah. That Jeroboam became outstanding in such an amorphous mass of conscripted labour, cursing, sweating and dying, testifies to the unusual industry and vigour housed in this coarse workman. And Solomon spotted him and advanced him. So Jeroboam became chief taskmaster over the levy from the Joseph tribes. This fired his ambitions. What is more, he soon found two levers to advance his position—internal squabbles between the tribes and general resentment of king Solomon's dreary labour drafts where men were treated no better than slaves. So rebellion was kindled in Jeroboam's mind, and, while he showed himself to king Solomon as his most energetic task-master, he also showed himself secretly to that labour force as their champion, waiting only for the moment when he could lift up his hand against the king.

And then the unexpected happened. A prophet took him aside and whispered in his ear, 'Thus saith the Lord, the God of Israel. Behold, I will rend the kingdom out of the hand of Solomon, and will give ten tribes to thee...' Jeroboam could scarcely believe his ears, but he did believe them. And you can be sure such a thrilling forecast of what the future held was whispered to an inner circle of associates on the understanding that it was not to be divulged to anyone. But it was, of course. It always is. And king Solomon heard, leaving no course for Jeroboam but to flee to Egypt, a price on his head.

Then the wheel of fortune turned again. King Shishak of Egypt was more then ready to hear of any plots against his rival, King Solomon. So Jeroboam climbed to royal circles, and according to the Septuagint, even married a princess.

Nothing remained now but to wait for the opportunity to strike. It came, not in Solomon's reign, but in the reign of his son, Rehoboam, an insensitive tyrant. The people rose in a body against him. It was Jeroboam's chance. He slipped across the frontier, headed the rebellion, split the kingdom in two and as a result of his *coup d'état*, found himself head of the ten tribes of Israel with a rival capital to Jerusalem at Samaria.

All this sounds so familiar we could believe we have heard it before. What we haven't heard is that *this revolution had divine* approval. Under Solomon Israel had become idolatrous and under his successor contemptuous of human rights, and the two are not unconnected. For that double apostasy the break-up of the State was certain. Ahijah the Shilonite prophesied it and Jeroboam the upstart workman was the instrument to carry it out. So the kingdom was divided. So a *coup d'état* was undertaken with divine approval. This is what the Bible says.

2 Three views of rebellion

So we come to the agonizing question—is it ever right to lift up one's hand against the king? Is it ever right to plot to overthrow the government by force? Is it ever a part of a Christian's duty to join a revolution?

(a) There are those who tell us it is *never right* to rebel. They point to the example of Jesus our Lord who suffered death rather than resist the Romans. He did not even campaign for the abolition of slavery, so widespread a system in his day. But can we argue from this? Was not his a special ministry, a unique ministry, a saving action for the world? How could he give himself to political action over matters that belonged only to the time and circumstances of his day? And the same applies to the Apostolic Church. If its mission was to testify to this same Christ as the universal Saviour, had it not to be independent of political involvement in first century social problems, of which, granted, there was no lack? Is there then a clear-cut argument to be derived from scripture that it is *never* right to be involved in any kind of rebellion? Can even Romans 13. 1–7 and 1 Peter 2. 13–17, the classical New Testament scriptures on this subject be pressed that far?

(b) At the opposite extreme are those who seem to be saying that to rebel against the government is *the most Christian action* with which it is possible to be associated. They see Jesus as a revolutionary. He was plotting to overthrow the establishment by championing those at the bottom of the social ladder, by using force to turn out the cheating traders from the temple market, and by sympathizing (as some assert) with the Zealot party dedicated to overthrow by force of arms the ruling party in the land, not stopping at blood. There are leading Christians who see Jesus as belonging to the company of Marx, Lenin, Mao, Castro, Ho Chi Minh and Torres. For some, it seems, it is impossible to be a Christian without being dedicated to revolution in the modern world. Out of this there has even developed a *theology of revolution.* Is it not hard, however, to resist the conclusion that political aspirations, some of which may indeed be justified, are actually being read back into the story of Jesus as we have received it, in order to seek justification for an extreme point of view?

(c) Is there *an alternative* to these extreme positives? It would seem from the story of Jeroboam the son of Nebat, who lifted up his hand against the king, and did so with divine approval, expressed through the mouth of God's prophet Ahijah, *that there are times* when *a revolution has to be.* But—and this is most important—like surgery, it is always bad that it has to take place, it is always the lesser of two evils.

Take this rebellion of Jeroboam's against Rehoboam. Suppose it had not taken place. Suppose Rehoboam, that half-heathen insensitive tyrant, set as king over Israel, had been allowed to continue with his realm intact, to what depths would Israel have sunk? On the other hand, what did the revolution actually achieve? Did the break-away kingdom aspire to greater heights than would otherwise have been the case? Was the true worship of God established in Israel? Were the rights of the common people assured? Revolutions certainly dispose of unwanted and unworthy rulers. They also dispose of injustices and problems. The disheartening fact however is that rulers there are still, and injustices there are still, and problems that press; what has happened is a *change* of ruler, a change of injustice, a change of problem, which no doubt provide solutions in the short term, but before long do not appear to accomplish much more than temporary relief.

3   The need for caution

Is it ever right then to lift up our hand against the king? According to the Bible there are times and circumstances where it may be right, but they are very rare indeed. So those who do rebel need to be very sure that the rebellion they plan really is less than the evil with which they are confronted, for rebellion is an evil. They need to be very sure that their rebellion is on behalf of the fundamental rights of man and not waged in order to substitute one political system which they judge to be preferable, or more profitable, than another. They need to be reasonably sure also of success, and that speedily, because revolutions have a way of destroying more than they produce.

All this reflects circumstances of crying seriousness. The questions involved are agonizing, firm answers exceedingly difficult to find. The terror is that there are people in today's world living with these nightmares. No sensitive man or woman living in the enormously privileged position of a secure state can afford to pontificate. All we can do is to set out the alternatives and point to what the Bible has to say—no, that is not all, we can pray for those faced with a revolutionary situation, we can pray that the right may prevail and too much (there will be some) suffering be avoided.

15 God's Placemen

1 Kings 18.13 (NEB) *Have you not been told, my lord, what I did when Jezebel put the Lord's prophets to death, how I hid a hundred of them in caves, fifty by fifty, and kept them alive with food and drink?*

I do not suppose we have heard, unless of course we know our Old Testaments unusually well; I do not suppose we know about this extraordinary act of bravery; or even the name of the man who carried it out; or what was his position in life. He was Obadiah, comptroller of the royal household in Samaria, the capital city of Northern Israel. At least that was the obvious part of his calling. Anyone who had anything to do with the palace of King Ahab would most certainly have come into contact with Obadiah, the comptroller of the palace. He would have his finger on most of the business that had to be handled. Obadiah was a public figure in Israel, a man to be reckoned with, a man no doubt of some presence, for a man lacking those natural qualities would never be elevated to such a position.

This then was the obvious part of his calling; what was *not* obvious, but which is one of the reasons why this story is told, is that this man, this royal servant, was one of God's placemen. He was placed there by God, for his own divine purposes. This is the subject to occupy our minds as we consider this man.

1   Surprising situations

First we need to notice that God's placemen may be found in most surprising situations.

Take Obadiah. He was master of King Ahab's household. Now, no king in Israel's history was so roundly condemned for what he did as was this occupant of the throne. Ahab brought about the unthinkable. He introduced Baal worship into the land with all its attendant cruelty and filthiness. It was Obadiah's calling to be in constant service *to this man.*

Even so, this is not half the story. Ahab had married the foreign princess Jezebel. That marriage was no doubt a *mésalliance.* No doubt Jezebel despised the little kingdom of Israel with its brand new capital up on the Samaritan hill completely innocent of any kind of maritime power such as her home country, Phoenicia, possessed. No doubt she half despised Ahab the king ruling halfcock (as she saw him), because baulked by a stupid regard for the Yahweh religion his people professed, a religion which replaced the passion of her own Phoenician fertility cult with boring, straight-laced Israelite morals. But Jezebel would show him. Jezebel would show the Phoenicians back home and the Israelites round about her what a woman could do given the chance. She made a start with ferreting out the priests of this Yahweh. Dead tongues would not condemn. And she would annex what properties she coveted to add to the grandeur of the palace; and pity any who tried to say her nay. This lioness, comparable only to Cleopatra and Catherine de Medici, was the dominant figure in the palace where Obadiah was comptroller. God's placemen, I repeat, may be found in most surprising situations.

Corrie ten Boom, in the gripping account of her arrest in Holland by the Nazis during the last war for sheltering Jews (*The Hiding Place*, Hodder & Stoughton 1972), has a chapter called 'The Lieutenant.' Taken one day from her cell in the Scheveningen prison she found herself led to a hut to be interrogated by a German officer wearing a beribboned uniform, a gun in his leather holster. Wearily the questioning dragged on according to the standard German technique, designed to elicit information about the hiding places of the Jews, but all with studious politeness. He even provided a chair on which his prisoner could sit and warmed up the fire. Fearing that these politenesses were a trap to

73

cause her to relax and confess, she answered warily. Suddenly the interview broke off but was repeated next day. In it a most surprising turn took place. Corrie ten Boom found herself testifying to her faith in Christ as the true light in a world of darkness. At which Lieutenant Rahms, the German interrogator, pulled down the visor of his military cap over his eyes, the skull and cross-bones glinting in the sunlight. Then in a voice that could scarcely be heard he said, 'What can you know of darkness like mine...' He dropped back into his official stance but some days later the unbelievable happened. Corrie ten Boom found herself escorted to a hut where her brother had been brought for the sole purpose that they might enjoy a few words together. Lieutenant Rahms stood apart, not to intrude on their intimacy, and when he snapped out that it was time to go he did not cut short the prayer Corrie's brother offered up for the safety of Lieutenant Rahms, his wife and family back in Bremen heavily bombed; nor did he mock. Was that German one of God's placemen, all unbeknowing?

2   The courage of God's placemen

Secondly (perhaps it scarcely needs to be said), God's placemen need a peculiar kind of courage.

Go back to Obadiah. Every day for him was like living on ice dangerously thin. Any time it might break and his end be swift. This woman, Jezebel, was restless with passion. Every opportunity she siezed to dazzle the court, if not the country, with her charm, her wit, her subtlety and her ruthlessness. Obadiah was responsible to the king, but he had need to know that behind the king stood the woman exercising the real power in the land.

And then the edict went out that all the prophets of the Lord were to be slain. Jezebel was having no dried up religious criticizing her morals! Obadiah, a God-fearer since his youth, had no power to rescind that order, but he trembled for the prophets. He trembled for the future of his country. What future indeed could there be if the word of

God was stifled completely? Conscience would almost fail to operate and justice lie in ruins. Israel had no prospects of survival unless it kept its strong distinctive religious character. Those prophets must somehow be saved, but how? Obadiah felt the terrible responsibility revolve upon himself. He alone, or almost alone, was 'in the know.' He alone from his privileged position could trickle out a desperate warning to the threatened prophets. He alone could divert attention from their hiding places. This he did and saved the lives of a hundred. And, if he scarcely slept at the thought of what he risked, who will dare to accuse this suave and cautious palace official of lacking cool and calculating courage?

Was it God's purpose that his prophets should be saved for the future? He had his instrument ready, his placeman in the royal palace, Obadiah, willing to risk his life to defend God's servants. It takes some courage to be God's placeman.

3   The responsibility of God's placemen

We have not quite finished this story. There was one man in Israel whom Ahab hated more than any other. It was Elijah. He hated him because he was convinced that he, Elijah, was responsible for the drought that was crippling the economy of his kingdom. How could Ahab build up his reputation when the crops were failing and their livestock dying off? How could he hold his own with Jezebel if he could not raise his stature by successful enterprise? Elijah was the culprit! Elijah revered by the people, and, if the truth were known, half revered by himself. But life with Jezebel goaded him. Elijah must die! But where was he? Not even Obadiah knew.

And then it happened. During a search for grass at the king's command to keep, if possible, the horses and cattle alive, Obadiah came face to face with Elijah who only had one word to say—'Go and tell your master that Elijah is here.'

Could we see Obadiah now I think we should see the blood drain from his face. 'What wrong have I done?' he protested. 'Why should you give me into Ahab's hands? He will put me to death... Have you not been told, my lord, what I did when Jezebel put the Lord's prophets to death, how I hid a hundred of them in caves, fifty by fifty, and kept them alive with food and drink? And now you say, "Go and tell your master that Elijah is here." He will kill me.'

There are times and there are situations when the most dangerous course is the timid one. If Pastor Niemöller had been less bold to confront Hitler with the truth of the gospel of Christ and what that gospel requires morally and ethically, there is no doubt that he would never have come out of his imprisonment alive.

Elijah had been hiding but when the time came to face the king he would face him and face him alone. Obadiah was bidden to deliver the message. And then this supreme playing down of all the characteristic played-down dramas which the Bible records we read, 'So Obadiah went to find Ahab and gave him the message.'

So this brave and faithful comptroller of the royal palace passes off the biblical record never to be heard of again. His little history there is overtaken by the great history of that stupendous contest on Mount Carmel ostensibly waged between Elijah and Ahab, but in reality between the God of Israel and the prophets of Baal battling for the soul of Israel. Let us be realistic. Over against this all that Obadiah did was small. But this is not the point. Obadiah was faithful and courageous *in the place where God had caused him to be.* That is enough. He was God's placeman and he did not fail. See him at the very last going to meet Ahab with the dangerous words on his lips, 'I have met Elijah.'

You may not be called to live out your Christian life as an archbishop, a cardinal, a moderator, a kind of Billy Graham or even a parish priest or pastor. You find yourself in an office where the conversation is sometimes lewd and the practices occasionally sharp. Or you are a housewife, secretary, a school-teacher, a civil servant or an engineer.

76

You could not probably make much of a claim for your Christian status in the world. Maybe not. Let us be realistic. *But you are God's placeman.* This is what the story of Obadiah tells you. You will need courage, courage simply to be what you are as a Christian where you are, and courage sometimes in an emergency when you least expect it.

Is your name Obadiah? I do not mean literally! I remind you he has an honoured place in the biblical record. He is not forgotten in the eternal reckoning. Neither will you be if you are faithful and courageous in your faithfulness.

16   God's Gospel, not Ours

2 Kings 7.9 (NEB) *What we are doing is not right. This is a day of good news and we are keeping it to ourselves.*

I can visualise someone switching off his attention because of this verse selected from the Second Book of Kings. The supposition is that what is to follow is a piece of fanciful forcing of an Old Testament scripture to suit a commonplace evangelical theme. I would be sorry were this to happen, not least because care has been taken to check the translation 'day of good news.' The Hebrew is *Yom Beshorah,* which the Septuagint puts into Greek as *Hemera evaggelias.* Even without a knowledge of Greek it is possible to hear the word 'evangel' in this. So we really do have an evangelical theme.

But what a setting! And what unexpected lessons come out of it.

A   The setting

First the setting. The king of Syria had lain siege to the capital city of Israel, that is, Samaria. To such desperate straits were the inhabitants reduced that even a donkey's

77

head and a handful of locust beans reached fantastic prices. Then there was that horrible scene of two women calling to the king as he walked along the city wall. 'Help, my lord king!' cried one of them. 'This woman said to me, "Give up your child for us to eat today, and we will eat mine tomorrow." So we cooked my son and ate him; but when I said to her the next day, "Now give up your child for us to eat", she had hidden him.' And before we write off this ghastly scene as utterly and completely outside the twentieth century, let me tell you that in the nine hundred days of the siege of Leningrad which began in 1941, starving men and women did not enquire into the nature of the ground meat patties that were on sale in the Haymarket at the fantastic price of three hundred and four hundred roubles for half a dozen or so. Corpses being dragged away on sledges for burial were not infrequently seen with the more fleshy parts cut off.

Overnight, however, the situation for the besieged city of Samaria dramatically changed. Suddenly the siege was lifted and the encircling armies hastily retreated, so hastily that they abandoned their tents and their provisions. The enemy encampments stood wide open for occupation by any who cared to enter. And four men did. They crept into tent after tent, dazed at what they saw, food in abundance, food sufficient to feed an army as indeed it had been doing. And, of course, they gorged themselves; and not only that, they took clothing and gold and silver, which they hid as provision for lean days ahead. Then their consciences smote them and they said one to another, 'This is a day of good news and we are keeping it to ourselves.'

B The lessons

And now the lessons. They are surprising.

1 The occasional evangelist

First we observe how these four evangelists, these bearers of good news, went, without waiting for the morning, to proclaim it to the watch over the city gate. To a starving city they said, 'There is food out there in abundance simply for the taking.' It sounded fantastic, but it was true. And in a way, the four evangelists (if that is what we are prepared to call them), were fantastic. They were outsiders, even outcasts, so diseased they were dangerous; but without preparation, without any kind of calling, and without even moral qualifications, they were the bearers of the good news, such good news that they saved a city. Do not miss the point. In the first place, these four men were thinking only of themselves. Their mind was primarily occupied with their own lucky break at discovering a deserted military camp. And when they decided to publish the good news of their discovery, they only did so because they feared the possibility of future punishment if they kept quiet. There was very little morality, let alone religion, in their decision, and certainly no consciousness of the will of God or of sharing the love of God for suffering men and women in a besieged city. Self preservation was their motive.

I see these four men then as *unintentional* evangelists. I see them as four men caught up in the purpose and will of God without their being aware of the size of the operation that was in hand. This sort of thing happens. General Dozier of the United States Forces in Italy gets taken prisoner by the Red Brigade, and when he is released by a brilliant effort of the Italian police, he bears his testimony to the reality of prayer to a secularized Western world which no longer believes in prayer. What trained and authorised evangelist would command so widespread a radio and television audience as this? And Mr Pyke, a business man, arrested as a spy in Iran, speaks on release, not only of prayer, but how there exists in his heart no hate for his captors who unjustly held him in gaol for months, and not even a mattress on which to sleep. What a proclamation in a world where hate is on the increase!

We organize our evangelistic campaigns, raise money, plan, publicize and promote—and who will affirm that we are mistaken?—but we do not always recognize that the sovereignty of God operates *even with respect to the publication of his own gospel.* He will cause it to be heard, received and lived by, when he will and by whom he will; and some of the occasions and some of the instruments are wholly unexpected.

2 The organized Church

Secondly, we observe that the good news had already been proclaimed but it had been disbelieved. Elisha, back in the besieged city had said, 'Hear this word of the Lord: By this time tomorrow a shekel will buy a measure of flour or two measures of barley in the gateway of Samaria.' He had said it to the king with his lieutenant in attendance. He had said it as the recognized upholder of the nation's faith. He, the official religious leader, had proclaimed the good news of God's ample provision for the needs of his people. But the king received the message in stony silence, and his lieutenant received it with open mockery. 'Even if the Lord were to open windows in the sky, such a thing could not happen!'

There come times when the official voice of a religious tradition is not heard. What we need to note is that the failure does not always lie in the corruption or weakness of that body, but in the unwillingness of the people to receive any message of good tidings from *organized* religion. Such a time is the present. While the main-stream Churches (as they are called), struggle in a climate of secularism and economic stringency, the free lance and the peripheral religious movements flourish, especially among the young.

Organized religion is not free from risks. Staleness, dull conformity and hypocrisies are ever present dangers. In Israel there were false prophets who spoke only smooth things to please the king and win popularity among the people. And there were time-serving priests concerned chiefly to 'line their own pockets.' Established Churches are always liable to these corruptions. But for all the risks, and they are real, there would be no religious faith to hand on from generation to generation without an organized Church. It is true that the faith has to come alive for each generation and in a form suitable for that generation; but, as lessons cannot be learned unless there is a school to learn them in, so the faith cannot be a living experience unless there is a Church to carry the burden of proclaiming it, in season, out of season, whatever the climate.

Of course there was something exciting about these four outcasts proclaiming the good news of plenty to a hungry city. Of course there is something exciting about some imprisoned criminal coming to the point of confessing a Christian faith, and let not its genuineness be questioned; but do not fail to hear the same good tidings which the Church has been proclaiming for generations. It is *this body* which carries the burden of responsibility for faith in the land.

3   God the sovereign employer

One more point. It concerns the king in this story. To appreciate it we must go back to that horrible siege situation. The king was walking along the city wall when a woman cried out to him for help. She had a perfect right to do this for he was the divinely appointed guardian of the city's welfare. What she actually said (in Hebrew) was, 'Save us, O king.' But he had no good news of salvation to offer. More than that he abdicated from his position of responsibility. 'If the Lord will not save you, how can I?' No wonder she went on to tell her repulsive tale of woe. Still he had nothing to offer, not even a word of sympathy, though he performed the ritual act of rending his clothes, and the people saw he was wearing sackcloth next his skin. To crown all, he vowed he would execute Elisha the prophet of God forthwith, counting him, and behind him *God*, as responsible for the city's plight.

So the king put himself over against God, instead of with God as his servant; and when Elisha proclaimed the good news of God's plenty, he had nothing to say, and when the four unintentional evangelists also proclaimed it, his immediate reaction was to dismiss it as a trick of the enemy.

Perhaps we ought not to pass harsh judgement on this king. The city's plight was desperate. There seemed no possible way in which relief would come. And when the news was proclaimed that the enemy had fled, in ordering an investigation to make sure that this was not a ruse to lure the besieged out beyond the walls where they could be massacred, he was not reacting beyond the reasonable and normal on the part of any military commander, Nevertheless, the blunt fact is he had replaced faith by doubt, and trust in God by rational considerations. For such, God has no more use. I do not for one moment mean by this that God has cast him off for ever. The love, mercy and compassion of God are far greater than 'the measure of man's mind.' I mean that if a man, if a servant of God, if a king, even a Church, comes to the point of abdicating from the stance of faith, that is, trust in God, he/it will be dropped from the working out of God's purpose in the world, he/it will be replaced by another, and those purposes will continue. So four outcasts motivated by nothing higher than their own safety, found themselves employed by God as the bearers of *his good news*. God takes up one and sets down another in his work of implementing his purpose in the world, including the proclamation of his gospel, for it is his.

Conclusion

There is enough in this story of the lifting of the siege of Samaria to sharpen in every servant of God, every worker for God, every Church, a sense of our dependence on him, effective so long as we stay in this position.

17.   Touching Bottom

Esther 9.13 (NEB) *Esther answered... 'let the bodies of Haman's ten sons be hung up on the gallows.'*

We touch bottom when we come to the book called Esther in the Old Testament. Indeed, it is difficult to believe that we are still in the same Old Testament that contains Genesis, Isaiah and the Psalms, when we turn to the work of this unknown author. Whatever made him put pen to paper for this brief historical novel (for this is what it is)? Whatever were the circumstances or intentions that made it possible for these ten chapters to be included in the Canon of Holy Scripture? There is scarcely anything moral about the book, let alone religious. God is not even mentioned, and there isn't one character that even begins to stir our admiration, unless it be Queen Vashti in the opening paragraphs, and she vanishes from the tale almost as soon as it begins.

1   The story

Maybe you have forgotten this story, if indeed you ever knew it, for it is not read in Church on Sundays. The stage is set in the reign of Xerxes (Ahasuerus in this book), whose vast domain stretched from Ethiopia to India with his capital at Susa. Here we are introduced to the king providing a banquet for his victorious army which was meant to be the utmost in splendour and lavishness. It went on for nights and days till it became, we may guess, a drunken orgy from which the court women thought it wiser to absent themselves. But the guests craved for sensual entertainment at their feast, something special, something fantastic, something never to be forgotten. Queen Vashti, a real beauty,

83

should parade before them all. Even the king commanded it. And if we imagine that what was in mind was some innocent, royal mannequin parade, we are too innocent to read this story. But Queen Vashti refused to come. She was not going to make an exhibition of her stunning form for the lewd satisfaction of a thousand drunken sots. All honour to her. Rather than forfeit her self-respect this woman endured the wrath of the king and was banished for life. One wonders what became of her.

Then there began a systematic sifting of all the pretty girls in Susa and beyond, to find a captivating substitute able to tickle the fancy of the king. His eye fell on Esther, a Jewish deportee and parentless, cared for by her cousin, Mordecai. Nothing, however, of her race and origin did king Xerxes know, and Mordecai pressed upon the girl not to ruin his chances and hers by divulging their secrets.

There was, however, at court one who not only knew, but nursed an inveterate hatred of the Jews, and especially of Mordecai, who persistently refused to accord him the respect others were in the habit of giving. His name was Haman, and like a snake in the grass he waited his opportunity, which came, and he took it. He saw to it that an edict was pronounced ordering the slaughter of all the Jews throughout the provinces and the confiscation of their property. There would be no escape from the thoroughness of this pogrom. It would catch Mordecai; indeed for him he had a seventy-five foot high gallows erected where he could watch his enemy's painful execution.

But he had reckoned without Esther, he had reckoned without her subtlety and the hold she exercised over the fascination of the king. Artfully she caught Haman in the trap he had set for Mordecai. In the end he swung from the very gallows he had contructed for his victim. What was more, the Jewish minority throughout the provinces was freed from the terrible fate poised over its head. So a day of rejoicing was kept, later known as the Feast of Purim. But then the story really does touch bottom. The liberated Jews took their revenge on their would-be persecutors, revelling in the slaughter they found themselves able to inflict, while Mordecai strutted forth in magnificence, the most honoured man in the kingdom, second only to the king.

2   What the message is not

What has happened that a low level story such as this should have found its way into the book we traditionally recognize as the word of God? And such the Bible is, including the Old Testament. It is the place where we hear God speaking to us if we listen with the ears of faith and expectancy.

I believe we are on the wrong track of the real message of this book of Esther if we go searching for isolated texts which we think can be puffed up to yield spiritual lessons for our day. An example is chapter 4, verse 14—'Who knows whether it is not for such a time as this that you have come to royal estate?' What we are looking at here is a bare residue of faith, and pretty bare it is. What we see in the book of Esther is a glimpse here and there of some dimly burning wick of genuine religion *all but extinguished*.

Look realistically at the situation as it is. Here is a young woman waiting to step into Queen Vashti's shoes, exiled because she wished to keep her self-respect. Here is a young woman whose religious faith means so little to her that she is ready to suppress the knowledge of it lest it jeopardize her chances of advancement in the king's obviously fascinated eyes. Here behind her is a man, her cousin, her guardian, reputed to love her as his own daughter, aiding and abetting her in this secrecy. Very well, let it be granted that she risked her life if she refused to succumb to the mighty king's sexual desires. Powerful overlords have always had a way of claiming what women they wished. English history will suffice to tell us this. But is there not the story of Daniel and his three friends also in the Bible? They risked death rather than even eat of the king's food; and Daniel went to the lion's den rather than suppress his Jewish form of daily prayer. Not so Esther. Not so Mordecai. There is not a breath of prayer in this story. There is no appeal of any kind to God to help.

All that is left of religion to Esther and her guardian is some kind of residual awareness that the Jews have a special place in history, that the Jews will somehow survive the calamities that overtake them, if not by means of one agency then of another, that failure to seize opportunities spells punishment, and that it is at least possible to raise the question that some form of providence may operate in the affairs of men and women. Add this together and it comes to little more than a vague belief in fate, even if labelled religious fate. All this is what makes me assert that in the book of Esther the magnificent faith of the Hebrew people in the living, forgiving, recreating God has touched bottom. And when we go on to read of the Jews in Susa killing five hundred people by way of revenge and Esther herself asking that Haman's ten sons be strung up on the gallows erected for Mordecai, we wonder if this woman set before us as the heroine in the book knew anything at all of the God who forgives even his persecutors.

3   The message

What then is this book of Esther for? It is not for me to attempt to answer the question, why was it originally included in the Canon of Holy Scripture. I ask, as a contemporary preacher, what does the book say to me now that it is in Holy Scripture? It says to me—be careful. Even the most inspiring and true religious faith, buttressed by ritual rites and ceremonies can run out into the sands of a vague belief in fate, opportunism and revengeful self-seeking. It is sometimes alleged that the confession of a faith leads to a clouded mind. This is possible if the object is unworthy, say a belief in some fetish, lucky charm, material gain, social advancement or a vague religious fate. But if the religious faith and practice is kept in vital touch with the living God made known to us in the total message of the Old Testament and above all in Jesus Christ our Lord, it is broadening, deepening, uplifting and energizing. Faith, hope and love mark it out as exceptional, and especially love, yes, even love of enemies admittedly only possible by the grace of God.

Poor Esther! Were you happy with your mighty Xerxes? Were you happy on all those occasions when other girls in the harem took their turn in the royal bed? Was it worth suppressing your racial origin and your religious faith to win this privilege? though of religious faith you had precious little. Poor Mordecai! Were you happy strutting around Susa with your golden crown, your gorgeous robes and everyone bowing low, O so low, whenever you passed along the street? Poor people of Susa and all the satrapies in the Persian kingdom! What a witness you might have had of the compassion of God if both Queen Esther and Deputy Mordecai had preached forgiveness from the very gallows Haman had erected on which to hang the Jews. But no! Vengeance won the day and the long knives came out. What a pity! That is the tragedy of the book of Esther. When religion touches bottom that alas is what we see. What can we do who read the book but pray:

'From all sedition, privy conspiracy, and rebellion;
from all false doctrine, heresy and schism;
from hardness of heart, and contempt of they word
and commandment,
Good Lord, deliver us.

(from the Litany. BCP)

18.   God Comes in the Dark

Job 2.9 (AV) *Dost thou still retain thine integrity?*
Curse God and die.

1   Hard questions

Would he, do you think? Would he die if he cursed God?
Would he, if out of all the pain, misery and loneliness of the
appalling collapse about his ears of everything he valued in
life—his health, his wealth, his home and his family—would
he suddenly or even slowly, fold up if he cried out that God
was a damned liar, a cheat or a tyrant worse than any Cyrus,
Ivan or Stalin, beating down the helpless? You know he
wouldn't! You have heard men curse God before now and
go on living, go on living defiantly, recklessly, yes and
profitably. So what is this woman talking about, 'Curse God
and die'?

First, I would have you notice that this is a woman
speaking. It is Job's wife. It is the person who lived closest
to Job and read Job, not only his actions but his motives, not
only his mind but his heart, not only what he said, but what
he thought, as only a woman can. She knew then about her
man's faith (more than perhaps he knew himself), she knew
how deep it was, how strong it was, how part of his very self
it was. This woman knew that for *this man* life without his
faith was impossible. There would be no life, no life that
could be called life, even though he might live physically,
only a living death, only a dragging around with emptiness
at the heart of everything. This is the terror of once having
been gripped by faith in the living God. You can never really
live again without it. 'Curse God and die' urged the woman.
Was she right or was she wrong? No, not was she right or
wrong to urge it, but was she right or wrong in her prophecy

88

of the consequence of cursing! I submit to you that she was dead right... *for Job.*

But was she right to urge it in the light of her conviction about the consequences? Was she right to urge that Job take his own life as a way out of his misery? Was she right to counsel a form of suicide? Was she right to press on her husband the strike weapon against God—'I won't damn well live if this is how you treat people!' Was she right to advocate a kind of 'Bobby Sands reaction' to a loathsome condition?

2 Love or principle

I reckon we need to pause here for a moment to consider this woman. Why did she say to her husband, 'curse God and die'? Was it not because her heart bled for him? Was it not that she could not bear another day to see him pitifully scraping those pitiful boils of his to ease a little his pitiful pain?—and all to no advantage. Oh, better die than this! Better be a widow in Israel, better a woman easy prey to all the rapacious, money-loving, lust-loving, hateful men in society than bear this pain another day of watching one you dearly love driven down to desperate degradation. I reckon we have assessed this woman shamefully if we do not assess her cry, 'curse God and die' as spoken out of love, love for her man who had given her everything in life she prized. But was she right to urge it? Let it be admitted that she spoke out of love, was she right to urge it? Is a course of action right simply because it has its roots in love? Does love justify *everything* we say or do? This is a hard question, but nothing like so hard as having to refuse a way out of a wilderness which love offers and to refuse it in order to maintain cold integrity. 'O, Lord, lead us not into temptation.'

And you will notice Job does refuse. No, I will not accept the words of refusal as set out in the New English Bible harshly, 'You talk as any wicked fool of a woman might talk.' No. No. No! The Authorized Version surely has it right. 'Thou speakest as one of the foolish women speaketh.' It is not like you to talk like this. You are putting yourself in the opposite camp where I know you do not belong, and I appreciate why you do it, and the cost to you, but what you counsel is wrong. 'Shall we receive good at the hand of God, and shall we not receive evil?' Come what may of darkness, doubt and despair, we must still trust God, for it is only by him we live at all.

We speak of Job's comforters in the story, who could not comfort because they were too shallow. Eliphaz the piously pompous, Bildad the narrowly orthodox and Zophar the blustering talker. Perhaps also Elihu, the young man who thought he knew all the answers. Four men! But I suggest there was a fifth comforter who offered the wrong comfort to a man in misery, a woman, this woman, his wife, but she spoke out of love only, and not from principle.

3   God takes the initiative

Time would fail us to survey the whole book of Job in the Old Testament. It must suffice to say that though refusing to curse God and die, and though not finding a satisfactory answer to all his tortuous puzzles about him, yet in the end *he was found by God* and lived again.

Notice this! He was *found by God*, and it came in the way he least expected.

Some time ago, a friend of mine told me of an experience of hers when she visited Jerusalem with a party of her students. It was terrible weather. The rain poured down as it normally does only in the tropics. And they came to Bethlehem. There of course they descended to the cave where the guides tell you the Christ was cradled. The place said nothing to my friend, nothing at all. There was no manger, no cattle, no resemblance to anything the gospel narrative depicts—only some tawdry candles and some rather gaudy pictures. Remember they were drenched to the skin, their hair hanging in long, soaking, if not dripping strands. What reaction would you expect? Suddenly, however, the girl next to her exclaimed how wonderful it all was for her, and how it made the faith come absolutely alive. And she was a girl so outside the Christian faith that she had been accustomed to absenting herself from the religious exercises of her community. 'And', said my friend, 'that experience of that girl has made a mark on my life which has changed me.'

My friends, we cannot reason, organize or engineer our way to God. Instead, God comes to us how and when he will, though it is right to prepare for his coming. But the gospel of St Luke tells us this coming may be as a burglar in the darkness. Do not in your fascination for the burglar image fail to notice the darkness. God comes to us when everything seems as dark as dark can be. Do not forget that. Hold on to it.

'O tarry thou the Lord's leisure:
Be strong and he shall comfort your hearts,
All ye that put your trust in the Lord'

19.   The Faithful Remnant

Isaiah 10.21 (RSV) *A remnant will return.*

I do not have to explain to a congregation such as this that the remnant is not a length of material, be it wool, cotton or terylene, but a company of people usually called 'the faithful remnant', one of the major points of Isaiah's prophecy—'a remnant will return.'

1   Always a remnant

So expressed it sounds indescribably dull; but nothing in the Old Testament is dull when seen in its context, the context is always pulsating with life. Here it is a king driven to near distraction by two contrary political policies which could constitute escape routes from a disastrous siege threatening his capital. No siege is ever contemplated with equanimity, be it Leningrad in 1941 AD, or Jerusalem in 735 BC. It is always terrifying. See then King Ahaz in this light. See him with his court examining the city's water supply to ascertain what chances there might be of holding out against the siege threatened by the armies of the North, should he refuse to join in their rebellion against Assyria. What should he do? Join the risky Northern rebellion, or throw his country on Assyria's protection? What would you do?

And now we see a man striding through the streets of Jerusalem bent on confronting the king in his agonizing dilemma. With him is a little boy, *his* little boy. What the future holds, be it devastating war or peace, is always a matter of vital concern for the rising generation, whether the weapons to be employed are the cruel three-manned Assyrian chariot or the modern neutron bomb. So Isaiah takes his little boy to meet the king, and the name of the little boy is *Shear-jashub*, which means—a remnant will return.

And this was Isaiah's message—'a remnant will return.' But Ahaz wasn't listening. Of what interest could a prophecy of what lay beyond catastrophe possibly be to a king concerned to *avoid* catastrophe, catastrophe *tomorrow*. Do not be hard on King Ahaz. Put yourself in his shoes. A king is responsible for protecting his people. But the truth is, Ahaz's mind and Isaiah's mind were operating on different levels. Ahaz was concerned with an immediate problem. Isaiah was concerned with the long line of God's dealings with his people in history, past, present and future; how God works by, with and through the minority that trusts him, the remnant, the faithful remnant, the remnant of faithful people in any age.

2   The Church

Is all this dull, indescribably dull? Perhaps I would find it so did I not see the faithful remnant here this morning. For this is what the Church is, the Church gathered around the Lord's table—God's faithful remnant. But when I put it like this and count myself as belonging to that remnant, I squirm. It sounds too conceited, too self-satisfied and smug to be tolerated. I find this doctrine of the remnant hard to take. I do not *want* to be separated from my fellow men. But there really is no escaping it. Like it or not, when our neighbours, colleagues in the office, or work-mates get to know we are Church-goers, they will set us apart. Being a Christian involves us in being different.

There are two possible reactions to being God's faithful remnant, both of them wrong. The one is shame and the other is pride. Take shame first. Someone makes a disparaging remark about the Church. We are not ready for it. We are caught off our guard. Yes, here in the Church we are confident in our profession of faith, but how different when surrounded by scoffers! Maybe we do not disown Christ like Peter in the court room the night before the crucifixion and say, 'I know not the man', but we let the occasion go, we observe a discreet silence. Truth to tell, we are a bit ashamed of being known as a churchman, and cowardice takes over.

Perhaps you appreciate now why I find the doctrine of the faithful remnant hard to take. It is because of the tension it produces between being proud of our faithfulness to God's calling over against the appalling moral breakdown and uncertainty in the world today and shame at being a churchman. This tension has been evident in the history of the Hebrew people, and in the Pharisaism of the New Testament period—either pride *or* loathing at being different from other peoples, and the longing to be accepted as other nations are accepted, and sometimes almost grovelling to obtain that acceptance. The Christian Church too has exhibited that tension. At one time triumphant with its impressive buildings, state connections and gorgeous ritual, at another time bending over backwards to show itself on the side of the poor and outcast and the refugees. It was never easy to be part of the faithful remnant, and it is not easy now. To get the balance requires all the wisdom of which we are capable, and all the grace that is available.

93

3   The future

But will God hold us safe, bungle as we are certain to do the fine balance of our calling? Yes, that too is certain. 'A remnant will return.' God will never leave himself without witnesses. So it has been throughout the whole of biblical history. Those of you who know your Old Testament will remember how, through unfaithfulness, the Northern Kingdom of Israel was rubbed off the page of history as an identifiable people in 721 BC, never to be heard of again. And the Southern Kingdom all but suffered a like fate in 597 BC for the same reason of unfaithfulness as a people of God; but in 537 BC a remnant *returned* from exile. And that remnant too became unfaithful. What more blasé attitude to religion can you read than that recorded of God's people in the last book of the Old Testament, Malachi; but even there a book of remembrance is written for those who 'think upon God's name.'

And the faithful remnant became smaller and smaller. It was T.W. Manson who taught that it dwindled down to one person only who was completely faithful, faithful when all forsook him and fled, faithful unto death, faithful even when apparently forsaken in death, Jesus of Nazareth; and true to promise, this faithful remnant returned from the exile of the grave. This faithful remant has grown into the minority that is the Church of this Christ, of which St Matthew must have prophesied the truth when he put down in black and white—'And the gates of hell shall not prevail against it.'

Conclusion

Ought we then to be ashamed to belong to the faithful remnant? Ought we not rather to be proud to belong? How shall we get the balance right? We shall accomplish it, I think, by keeping our eyes steadily on the faithful remnant *par excellence*, Jesus Christ our Lord, who walked humbly with God, but was never treated by men as of no account. God's servant (and that includes you and me), is after all, the servant of the most high God, nothing more than a servant, but nothing less than 'of the most high God.'

20.   Our Redeemer is the Creator

Isaiah 44.24 (NEB) *Thus says the Lord, your ransomer, who fashioned you from birth: I am the Lord who made all things, by myself I stretched out the skies, alone I hammered out the floor of the earth.*

During the time even of the youngest worshipper in this Church, let alone those well past middle life, there have taken place the most fantastic advances in technological expertise. No one but a fool or an ignoramus would deny this. From agriculture with its new astonishing grain yields to space travel, to heart transplantation, to satellite communication systems, to word processing, to computer information banks, the skill of man seems boundless. There appears to be nothing, given time, he will not be able to accomplish.

1   Human limits

When however we stop to think, the skills of man are not boundless. Apparently there are accomplishments beyond his reach. One is man's inability to stave off death; he may delay it, ease it, but stop it he cannot. Another is his lack of power to initiate life; he may redirect it, manipulate it, even at its point of origin, but to bring it into being is beyond him. And there is a claim not even man in his most expansive mood will make, which is that he made, or could make, the world. He has to take it as given. Possibly he could destroy it, he may indeed destroy it, but there is still the universe which he can neither destroy nor create. Here is a fact which cannot fail to expose our human limitation—space. Go out and look up at the night sky. The knowledge that that galaxy of stars and planets, which we can only partly see, is but one of a galaxy of galaxies, makes even *the thought* of man being able to make all this ridiculous. Man's skills are clearly not limitless. There is a point at which we can go no further. There are buffer stops to human expertise.

What is our reaction when we come face to face with these limits? Imagine yourself in some beautiful and extensive parkland. You wander all over it, enjoy it, develop it, even revel in it. Eventually, however, you come to a fence beyond which it is impossible to proceed further. You walk along by it. There are no gaps. You come to a gate but it is securely locked. What next? Do you say to yourself, 'O well, there are interests, occupations and even pleasures enough within the enclosure. I will trouble myself no more about the fence.'? Is not this the line most of us pursue?

2   Questions and attitudes

Alright, we cannot prevent death, we cannot initiate life, we did not, cannot, fashion the universe; but there is still 'match of the day' to watch on the television, there is still the task of raising the mortgage payments, there is the summer holiday to plan with or without Sir Freddy Laker's assistance. What is more, this tacit acceptance of the frontiers of our human endeavour works for most of us for most of the time *until*—yes, until—something desperate eats into our complacency about ultimate questions. We stand guilty of some disgraceful offence, a bereavement opens an entry into bitter loneliness, a hopeless illness is diagnosed. What then? We stare at the fence. How did we arrive in this wretched enclosure? *Why* did we arrive here? What is the point of existence anyway? Whose is this parkland we have enjoyed and wish to enjoy?

There are *three possible attitudes* to these awkward questions. One is to shrug the shoulders with the confession, we do not know. This is the way of agnosticism, which at least has this to its credit, that it is a humble attitude.

Then there is the theory that the whole universe is the product of chance. This attitude may be left in the vaguest of terms where, with the increase of our knowledge of the wonders of the natural world, it becomes more and more incredible. Or it may be scientifically expressed in terms of the random associations of basic elements. These hypotheses are atheistic and on this account less humble than the agnostic.

The third alternative is the leap of faith, it is the attitude which believes in a divine creator whose mind and purpose lie behind all that is. It does not rest on logical proof but neither is it destructible by logic proof. It accords with the mystery of human experience and is demonstrably an uplifting and energizing stance. Faith in God as creator is creative. Men and women of faith are generally more purposeful than those of unfaith. When we cease to believe in anything we flag.

3 The Creator is the Redeemer

So we come to our text from Isaiah 44.

> 'Thus says the Lord, your ransomer,
> who fashioned you from birth:
> I am the Lord who made all things,
> by myself I stretched out the skies,
> alone I hammered out the floor of the earth.'

It is important to observe that this is no academic hypothesis. It is not a statement made in a theological classroom. On the contrary, it is an address by a national figure to a people wrestling with the second largest crisis of their peoples' history, the second exodus. Not the exodus from Egypt which formed the foundation of the nation's life, but the exodus from Babylon where pride, identity and faith were all but broken on the wheel of military defeat, deportation and exile. But the day came when the survivors were free to go home. The releasing edict was signed and promulgated. Between exile and home, however, lay a wearisome desert to be crossed. And at journey's end, what? A temple in ruins! Towns and villages heaps of stones! Once fertile agricultural land ruined by enemy occupation! Was the second exodus worth the effort? Put yourself in their shoes. To such a situation as this the prophet spoke:

> 'Thus says the Lord, your ransomer,
> who fashioned you from birth:
> I am the Lord who made all things,
> by myself I stretched out the skies,
> alone I hammered out the floor of the earth.'

This is the point at issue. If we are to be lifted out of the crippling defeats of human experience, if we are to gird up our loins and make the effort required to triumph over hardship and frustration, we must believe in something, but it must be something beyond ourselves and beyond our own fashioning. Man's expertise, man's accomplishments, have limits. There is a fence beyond which he cannot operate and there are times and places where the fence is closer to us than in our expansive moments we even guess. This is why the prophet pointed the dejected exiles to the great Creator as the means to pull them out of their dejection. This is why, too, in these same chapters of Isaiah there is an extended lampooning of idol manufacture. Nothing we can make, not even religious ideologies and rituals, can ransom us from captivity to ourselves. But the Creator can set us free and wills to set us free, but we must recognize his existence, we must accept the words of this prophet.

> 'Thus says the Lord, your ransomer,
> who fashioned you from birth:
> I am the Lord who made all things,
> by myself I stretched out the skies,
> alone I hammered out the floor of the earth.'

4 The Redeemer is the Creator

It is to be wondered if we Christian people have always seen our redemption against this giant canvas of creation. May it not be that we have viewed Christ, our acknowledged redeemer apart from creation altogether? In which case what happens is that our religious faith grows sickly as a kind of exceptional, even hot-house plant. The fourth gospel should have warned us. It reads, 'The Word, then, was with God at the beginning, and through him all things came to be; no single thing was created without him. All that came to be was alive with his life, and that life was the light of men.' And then this first chapter of St John proceeds to our redeemer. 'So the Word became flesh; he came to dwell among us, and we saw his glory, such glory as befits the Father's only Son, full of grace and truth.'

Our Redeemer is the Creator, the Creator is our Redeemer. This is the great truth to which the Bible bears witness. Hold to this and the faith evoked will be no pokey, restricted, narrow minded, ghetto-conditioned squint, but an intelligent commitment to the vastness of the divine mind, heart and purpose traceable in his created universe and brought home to us in his Christ.

I have made the point that the Bible bears witness to the great truth that our redeemer is the creator and the creator is our redeemer. It is the crowning message of the Old Testament when it reaches its height in these chapters of Isaiah from which my text was taken.

> 'Thus says the Lord, your ransomer,
> who fashioned you from birth:
> I am the Lord who made all things,
> by myself I stretched out the skies,
> alone I hammered out the floor of the earth.'

If then Christ is our redeemer, and no one who bears the name of Christian can believe less, how can he be a creature like the rest of us however highly we elevate him in our esteem? Must we not go along with the Church's traditional conviction that the Incarnation is true? Our redeemer is the creator.

21. Facing Failure

Jeremiah 20.18 (JB) *Why ever did I come out of the womb? To live in toil and sorrow and to end my days in shame!*

One afternoon a few years ago I found myself in the position of chairman of a selection committee. It was my responsibility to put forward a name for a job vacancy. There were a number of applicants out of which a short list of possibles was drawn up. They were invited to attend an interview. Each of them showed himself keen for the job, one or two so keen I feared for the disappointment they would experience if they failed to get it. And of course all but one would fail. All but one would receive from me the letter saying I was sorry but someone else had been offered the job and had accepted it. And when those letters were posted I wondered how they would be received. How would these recipients face failure? I hoped there might be someone around to help them take it. It is hard to take failure. As it happened, I heard how one of them had taken it very badly indeed.

I wonder if I am addressing someone who has never had to face failure! Someone who has passed every examination he has ever sat, whose business has prospered, whose marriage is as happy as can be, whose family has grown up to be a real credit to the parents, whose health has never once let him down; honours have even come his way, with the attendant public recognition. There are those for whom this certainly appears to be the case, though of course the outside world never knows what skeletons stand within the domestic cupboard. For most, however, failure is part of life's experience, and for some, a *life of failure*. The Old

100

Testament brings one such to our attention—the prophet Jeremiah.

A   Jeremiah, the man

Jeremiah was a shy, sensitive man whose unexpressed hopes would have been met by a quiet rural life on his property at Anathoth, a few miles north of Jerusalem. His forbears had dwelt there continuously ever since one of them, the only famous one, had been banished there by King Solomon for backing his rival to the throne of King David, his father. Jeremiah had no wish for the court life where his illustrious ancestor had fought and failed, no hankering after city life, no day dreams of publicity and nationwide recognition. For him 'the trivial round and common task' which care of his property required, was all he asked. It provided the background for his real love—the exercise of his superb poetic gift, the skill to capture with fascinating words, the ever changing patterns of the world of nature which pressed upon his keen observation and finely tuned spirit in his beloved Anathoth. See him striding across the fields, now stopping to watch and listen, there you have Jeremiah, a lonely man, refined, and seeking nothing for himself. Only the few would appreciate such a man as this.

And then wholly unexpected, and if the truth must be told, wholly unwanted, the call came to Jeremiah to be a preacher of what is right and wrong, not only in private but in public life—the thing he hated. No one can tell exactly how the call came, except to note that it was through two pedestrian visions of an almond tree and an overturned cooking pot. But however it came, it thrust him out, not only on to a public platform he loathed, but the public platform of the capital city, clashing, for ever clashing with kings, courtiers and priests. And not only this, but to execute that unwanted ministry without support of family, wife or children, a man utterly alone. And as if that was not sufficient, to *fail* in his ministry, receiving no rewards but mockery, persecution and exile, till finally the curtain fell upon his shrunken life

101

somewhere in Egypt, a martyr to the people he never ceased to serve.

I warn you, I doubt if you will warm to Jeremiah, few people do. But, inasmuch as the sour taste of failure does not altogether miss our palates, we ought not to turn down without more ado the sorrowful picture of this sorrowful man, of whom, strangely enough, yet perhaps not so strange, the people of Galilee were reminded when they encountered Jesus of Nazareth six hundred years later on. There are lessons here.

B   Lessons from Jeremiah

1   Concerning our characters

First perhaps, *the lesson that failure tests the strength of our characters.*

I have been reading the story of a young mother in Dublin, to whom was born in 1932 a victim of cerebral palsy. Unable to speak or control his limbs, there was no sign that an intelligent or sensitive being inhabited that tortured, mis-shapen little body. Yet the mother never ceased to believe that such existed if only it could be found. In spite of having a husband (a bricklayer) and a large and lusty family to care for, she gave time every day attempting to bring even a glimmer of recognition to the pictures she showed him and the songs she sang. All however failed. For five years they failed. She could not always stifle her tears over those failures. Yet this went on till one day with his left foot she saw the child deliberately pick up a piece of chalk. That was the start of a climb which took years to bring him to a useful life. The child grew to be a successful artist and playwright.

How many of us possess the strength to go on in the face of failure, perhaps years of failure? How easy to give up at the first difficulty, to relapse in to self-pity, to grow resentful of those more fortunate than we seem to be. How easy to become bitter with life in general and God in particular. Even in the realm of sport there are bad losers, and in politics, leading men who make an exceedingly poor showing in electoral defeat.

It may be that some of us have not yet learned to look upon failure as an ingredient of character building. But to whom would you go in a time of personal crisis—the man or woman who has had it all easy, or the one who has faced failure without giving up? You know who is the greater character.

I have encountered in my time men, successful men, some with first class brains, commanding presence, yes, even churchmen, on whose door I would not knock if I were in trouble. They would not understand. They have been too successful. They have never known the sour taste of personal failure.

During the last war a motor torpedo boat spotted six survivors clinging to a drifting life raft off Tobruk, their vessel having been sunk by an enemy dive-bomber. They were more like corpses than survivors. But when the crew of the salvage boat began to haul them aboard, one cried out, 'Wait, not yet.' Across his legs lay a seaman slowly dying. It was probably only a few minutes they had to wait, but it seemed like hours. When it was all over he climbed aboard and simply said, 'It was his first trip under my command.' Not till a month later did he add, 'He was my young brother.'

Strength of character comes to those who face with courage and say little, the tough patches in life, and one of the toughest is failure. The book of Jeremiah reminds us of the necessity to face up to this, if ever we are to be men and women of character.

2   Concerning our friendships

Secondly, failure tests our friendships. I still remember with some sense of shame—though there is nothing I can do about it after all these years—how I failed a friend because he had failed. We were students together, and I was

103

reminded of him not so long ago with the news of his death on the other side of the world. Possessed of a pleasing, if somewhat slow manner (which caused him the nickname of 'Dozey'), but an accomplished athlete, especially at Rugby football, he began to fail his college examinations one after another. This separated us. Then something happened—I do not know what it was—but he might have been 'sent down.' I regret to admit I did not befriend him then. I should have done. There is a saying, 'You can tell your friends when things go wrong.' If my fellow-student knew this saying, he could, I fear, have applied it to me. I know it now and am sorry.

Jeremiah knew it. As far as may be gathered from the book which bears his name, apart from the coloured man who pulled him up out of the water cistern when his enemies attempted to drown him, he possessed only one friend, his scribe, Baruch, whom he picked up in Jerusalem. This faithful man stood by Jeremiah through every failure, even rewriting the whole of Jeremiah's prophecies when King Jehoiakim, incensed by the contents, destroyed the scroll by dropping it in the fire. And what is more moving than that modest word of thanks to Baruch by Jeremiah at the close of his book?

'You do not know who your friends are till things go wrong.' Failure tests our friendships.

3 Concerning our faith

Thirdly, failure tests our faith. How Jeremiah's faith must have been tested! How often, up against the pattern of repeated failures which his life produced, must he have doubted the loving kindness of God ever to call him to be a prophet! And of these struggles we are left in no doubt, for unique in his book are those outcries (sometimes called Confessions), which let us peer into the travail of his soul where he was hardly satisfied. Not content with the cruel question, *Why?* he even cursed the day of his birth, and in at least one terrible failure of common compassion, cursed

104

his enemy with diabolical ferocity. Even the worm will turn!

But he that is without sin in questioning the worthwhileness of faith in God when all it appears to bring is failure, let him cast the first stone. I will not. Perhaps we can be grateful that Jeremiah lets us see him at his worst as well as his best, for the knowledge of it brings him closer to ourselves. Yet for all this Jeremiah never did desert. He stayed with his ungrateful people to the end and kept his faith, proclaiming it till (we may suppose), it cost him his life somewhere down in Egypt.

And was it a mistake that Jeremiah was called to this life and death of martyrdom? Can we not see that he was allowed to experience every prop to the formal religion of his day being kicked away, so that in sheer desperation he might reach out to the profound truth that the heart of religion is in the heart and not in forms and ceremonies. So he climbed out to a place no one had climbed before, and proclaimed there the new covenant, than which is nothing more striking in the Old Testament.

'The time is coming,' says the Lord, 'when I will make a new covenant with Israel and Judah. It will not be like the covenant I made with their forefathers when I took them by the hand and led them out of Egypt. Although they broke my covenant, I was patient with them, says the Lord. But this is the covenant which I will make with Israel after those days, says the Lord; I will set my law within them and write it on their hearts; I will become their God and they shall become my people. No longer need they teach one another to know the Lord; all of them, high and low alike, shall know me, says the Lord, for I will forgive their wrongdoing and remember their sin no more.' (31. 31– NEB)

And there came a day when a greater than Jeremiah, seated at a table with twelve men, one a traitor, reached out his hand as it were, and greeted his predecessor of long ago, echoing his words, 'This is my body, this is my blood of the covenant, shed for many for the forgiveness of sins.'

105

Failure tests our characters, our friends and our faith. It can be the raw material of our subsequent strength. Is not this the message of Jeremiah's illustration from the shapely vessels coming off the potter's wheel? In their making, the clay frequently failed and broke, but it was remade into a better vessel. All great lives have this as their secret. They have faced and incorporated into themselves the bitter experience of failure and been enabled to do so because they believed in the promised forgiveness of God.

22 Christian Non-conformity

Daniel 1.15 (NEB) *At the end of ten days they looked healthier and were better nourished than all the young men who had lived on the food assigned them by the king.*

In the year 597 BC fifty thousand Jews, including women and children, were driven out of their homes in and around Jerusalem, and marched across the desert to what we now know as the frontier of Iran and Iraq. How they survived at all is a mystery, but this would have to be said about the Jews in many other periods of their history, not least our twentieth century. When they arrived at their destination (or what was left of them, for hundreds must have dropped out of the march and perished in the sand), they were doubtless herded into concentration camps. It is a sickening story, and no less sickening for its repetition in the history of the Jews, time and time again. Man's inhumanity to man is, always has been, appalling.

1 The hard question

There came a day, however, when not only were the harsh conditions of the exiles eased and they were allowed to build houses of their own and plant gardens, but the king, knowing that he had collected in his concentration camps the cream of society from Jerusalem, despatched one called Ashpenaz to look out among the prisoners possible material (as we might say), to grace his court. They had to be of the blood royal and of the nobility, good-looking, intelligent and with courtly manners. So it was that four young men found themselves picked out for grooming for royal service. What were they to do?

Put yourself in their shoes. The king had defeated their country in war, cruelly driven them from their homeland, settled them in foreign territory where they could not even speak the language and where the life style repelled them. Moreover, Babylon, where the king's palace was, displayed a magnificence unsurpassed even by Athens or Rome. What were these four young men, whose diet, even, was utterly different, let alone their religion—what were they to do? Were they to accept the king's offer. Put yourself in their shoes!

You may be wondering why I am recounting the story of events that took place two thousand five hundred years ago. You might as well ask why the first chapter of the book of Daniel is appointed to be read in the course of public worship, because manifestly it is. I suggest as one answer that everyone in the modern world who calls himself a Christian is in some sense wearing the shoes that these four men had to wear. What were they to do, what are you and I to do?

2 Enter into life

First of all we note that they accepted the king's invitation. I cannot tell you if they sat up all night turning the problem over in their minds. I cannot tell you if they paced up and down the room as some of us know only too well when we have to face a crisis. I cannot tell you if they swallowed hard when they gave their assent, but gave it they did. So they were transferred from the boredom of prison to the brilliance of a palace.

What is the Christian today to do? Is he to contract out of public life because it is difficult? Is he to be a recluse, a stay-at-home, a mere back seat holder because the tempo of the modern world is laced with coarseness, permissiveness, blasphemy and greed? Is the Christian to play no part in the technological advance upon which the future of this country depends? Is he not to engage in the arts and sciences, if possible at the highest level? Is no Christian girl to go on the stage? Is a householder not even to own a television set because so many of the programmes are trivial, vulgar and violent?

The book of Daniel suggests the answer yes—the Christian should enter fully into the life of the world, and this doubtless includes its politics as well as its commerce and its culture; *but*, at the same time, it suggests that the Christian will need to be prepared at some cost, at some risk perhaps, to stand by a way of life different from the world in which he lives. A Christian is called to be the world's non-conformist.

3   The call to be different

Come back to this story. These four young men had to be groomed for the royal service. It meant instruction in the literature and language of the Chaldeans. No problem there. But what about the daily allowance of food and wine from the royal table? Jews have no preference for poor food, no preference for water instead of wine. I know! Not long ago, at someone else's expense, I stayed for a few days in one of the best hotels in Jerusalem. But the king of Babylon would not supply these men with *kosher* food. Even so, I doubt if this was the main problem. Those who have read something of what a Roman banquet was really like (hasn't the London stage recently been giving a sex-ridden society some idea—to the disgust of Mrs Whitehouse?) would know that what went on at pagan royal feasts was the real difficulty. It was filthy. So these four young men took their courage in their hands and declined the royal provision. Instead they lived on vegetables and water, and that in a king's house.

And now at last my text. 'At the end of ten days they looked healthier and were better nourished than all the young men who had lived on the food assigned them by the king.' (Daniel 1.15).

What is this verse saying? That vegetables and water should comprise our sole diet? I do not think so. What the text says to us is that, though the disciplines of the Christian way of life *are* demanding, costly and sometimes risky in a climate of looseness, greed and 'anything goes', which is characteristic of our time, it produces people far superior to those who let things slide, and simply do as Rome does. And the superiority is first apparent in the intellect, but it extends even to the physical appearance. It was not for nothing that the Christian Church introduced into its way of life very early on, days of fasting. The end in view was the sharpening of the mind. And a few days ago I came across this fact, that in the officers' prisoner-of-war camps in Germany during the last war, the meagre rations, when not too meagre, produced a higher level of mental activity than when the officers were well fed.

4   The value of discipline

The whole of the Western world today, and this includes our own country, finds this a hard lesson to take. Personal discipline is out and easy-go is in. Appetites must be nourished at once, whether for food, drink, sex, travel or time off, not least with the underlying assumption that this makes for the better life, the fulfilled life, the self-satisfying life. But does it? Now that discipline is almost a dirty word, is Europe a happier place? Is it a more peaceful place? Is it a safer place?

I do not think our text from Daniel can be made to recommend discipline for its own sake, but for the results it produces. These four men acquired a reputation as *outstanding men*, and you can be certain this included charm of manner and style as well as intellectual skill.

But what has this to say to us as Church people? This I think. That there is no need for us to be ashamed of our *disciplined* life. There is no need for us to feel a sense of inferiority because we do not swim with the tide. There is no need for us to imagine that we cannot possibly get out of life what unbelievers get out of it. We can lift up our heads. We can lift up our hearts. There is a place for humility, but there is also a place for confidence. And I will remind you where it is—in God, who, through his son Jesus Christ has *called* us to be his disciples in this place where we live and work and play. It is no small matter to be called to witness to Christ's disciplined way of life. Let us walk in it with a firm tread. It is the right way; and at the end of the day, and long before the end of the day, it will bring the deepest satisfaction. This is a lesson from the first chapter of the book of Daniel well worth learning.

23. A Man with a Grievance

Jonah 4.9 (JB) '*I have every right to be angry . . .*'

I wish I could draw. If I could I would draw a picture of Jonah slumped on the ground with elongated face, drooping mouth and fierce, blazing eyes. I am sure artists with catoonists skills must have attempted this. I wonder what would be your representation of a man with a grievance spouting out his angry disgruntlement with the words, 'I have every right to be angry, to the point of death.'

1 Jonah became small

But let us get down to the occasion. What is Jonah's grievance? Why is he so angry? You can scarcely believe it, but it was all about a castor oil plant, what the Authorized Version calls a gourd. It had grown up rapidly in the place where he was ekeing out his mood of bitter resentment, providing welcome shade from the fireceness of the near Eastern sun and the hot scorching wind. Then a worm got at it and it withered. The withering of that castor oil plant was the last straw. 'I have every right to be angry,' he said, 'to the point of death.'

When any one of us explodes over a little thing, it is usually because there is some large thing behind it. And that large thing, or series of large things, has set up an attitude, an attitude of resentment, if not of fierce anger. 'I have every right to be angry, to the point of death.'

(a) You might think from this that Jonah was a small man, the sort of man who easily takes offence, one almost looking for something at which to take umbrage. And he was a small man in a way, but not so small that God had not called him as decisively as any prophet to go and proclaim the message of God's concern for the heathen city dwellers of Nineveh. Jonah had something about him, to be entrusted with such a momentous assignment. He did not go of course, not at first, anyway. His attempted escape in a ship bound in the opposite direction from Nineveh, namely to Tarshish. The shipwreck and the swallowing up of Jonah, not by the raging sea, but by a roaming whale, is the part of Jonah's story most people know (if they know it at all), and unfortunately the point at which they withdraw serious interest—to their loss, I may say!

(b) And not only was Jonah of sufficient stature to be called to a significant mission, he knew 'in his bones' that, however frequently God might appear as a God of judgement, yet he was actually a God of infinite compassion. You can search the Old Testament and maybe the New, and you will not find a description of the heart of God to surpass that which

111

Jonah uttered, slouched in high dudgeon on the east side of Nineveh. 'I knew that you were a God of tenderness and compassion, slow to anger, rich in graciousness, relenting from evil.' Words the prophet Joel also used, making clear that if Jonah did not know them 'in his bones', he knew them as part of the general prophetic teaching. Jonah belonged to the prophetic circle.

(c) And Jonah was no mean preacher. Jonah could get his message across to complete outsiders, which is something not all our preachers can do. Nineveh was stirred to the depths by what they heard from the lips of this man, which, though a message of judgement, must somehow have been radiant with hope. The Ninevites repented, they turned to God and experienced his deliverance.

So we have to expunge from our estimate of Jonah the idea that he was basically a small man. There was the potentiality, and therefore the possibility of greatness in him! But he *became* a small man, so small that the last we see of him is someone slumped with elongated face, drooping mouth and fierce, blazing eyes, with that withered castor oil plant beside him, if not the worm that nibbled through its stem; a ripe subject indeed, for a cartoonist, and the bitter words blurting out from his lips, 'I have every right to be angry, to the point of death.'

2   Jonah's real trouble

How do you handle a man nursing a grievance? It is quite clear what you would like to do. You would like to approach him softly and inquire—'What is wrong, Jonah? Why are you so angry? It can't really be on account of that castor oil plant or that wicked worm!' You might get your head bitten off, of course. People with grievances are notoriously snappy. And then the truth came out. It was *God* Jonah was angry with. God, whose ways were not Jonah's ways, nor his thoughts Jonah's thoughts. Jonah did not see how he could get along with a God who showed up as he had shown up in Jonah's experiences. To put the matter crudely, though

112

maybe clearly, Jonah was 'fed up' with God, fed up, as we say, 'to the back teeth.' Thinking about God as he slumped there in the blazing sun and scorching wind, his shade gone, he grumbled, 'I have every right to be angry, to the point of death.'

3 Is this our picture?

Is this a picture of a rare phenomenon—a man angry with God because of the deal life has made out to him? No doubt this story of Jonah is a fictional piece of writing, but does it not tell the truth? Does it not tell the truth as a great masterpiece of painting tells the truth? Does it not tell the truth about people, about people in relation to God, about people when things do not go their way? May it not be telling the truth about us? This is always the terror of scripture. It acts like a sharp, two-edged sword, and sword thrusts hurt.

Here is a man declared redundant in his work, a good and honest employee. Here is a mother, a wise, careful, God-fearing mother, and her child is born with such a brain defect that he is almost an idiot. Here is a professional man, near the top of his professional tree, and he makes one unfortunate error of judgement which means his premature retirement from the stage of affairs. And the cry goes up, 'It isn't fair. What have these people done to deserve this?' It isn't as if they were bad people, careless people, even small-minded people. They have hearts and heads and hands above the average—but God apparently (yes, it is true), does not put a safety net under every one of his servants. So is it a rarity to find people slumped down with drooping mouth and fierce, blazing eyes? 'I have every right to be angry, to the point of death.'

I read a book recently, entitled *Undefeated*, by Lin Berwick (Epworth Press, 1980), with a Foreword by Andrew Cruickshank. If any girl might be thought to justify the querulous complaint, 'I have every right to be angry', it might be this East Ender. Born a hopelessly incapacitated

113

spastic, nevertheless, with the astonishingly patient as-sistance of her parents, she struggled to make something of her life, and did. Then in her teens came the doctor's report that she was gradually going blind. For the mother this was almost the last straw. Then, however, a young man, also incapacitated, brought new life by loving her, but after a while he grew weary of her incapacities and told her so. After this the parents' house was burgled and all the girl's records, tapes and playing equipment by which she made some contact with the artistic world, were smashed. Did she nurse a grievance against anyone? Against life? Against God? There is no sign of this. What is most remarkable, she actually came through to a practising Christian faith and finally took the step of confirming it and being confirmed in it in St Matthew's church, Poplar. Far from nursing a grievance, Lin Berwick came to nurse a faith.

'I have every right to be angry.' Yes, maybe you have, at the way life has treated you, even at the way *God* has apparently treated you. But is it wise to be angry? Is it ever right to be angry? You say, 'Our Lord was angry', but never on behalf of himself, only on behalf of other people. Yet he of all people might have had more cause to be angry than Jonah. He was called to proclaim God's love in Galilee and, before a few months were out, even the religious leaders of his day were plotting to do away with him; and they accomplished it. True, there was that one cry from the cross, 'My God, my God, why . . .?' but even then he did not look back in anger, he forgave.

Application

There are two keywords which cover the only attitudes which operate to raise us above defeat by the 'changes and chances of this mortal life.' They are *acceptance* and *faith*. Both are hard, very hard indeed in some circumstances. But, if we do not adopt them, we relapse into the slumped position of Jonah—a man with a grievance, a caricature of what he might have been and what we too might be; and that is a thousand pities.

24   Scattered and Gathered

Zechariah 10. 9–10 (JB) *I have scattered them among the peoples, but from far away they will remember me (they will teach their sons, and these will return). I mean to bring them back . . .*

Every Friday evening in one of the eleven houses that comprised the little cul-de-sac close by Kensington Gardens where we lived for almost twenty years, lighted candles seen through the windows marked it off as different. It was different. A well known Jewish family lived there.

I was brought up as a boy in an East Anglian town. There was nothing cosmopolitan about this place. It was solidly white, solidly English, solidly East Anglian—at least for all I knew. Ah, but there was one boy in my school called Finkelstein; quite popular he was, usually known as Finkey. He did not turn up on Saturdays. He was a Jew.

1   God's scattered people

In the little book of Zechariah in the Old Testament, we hear, as it were, the voice of God speaking. 'I have scattered them among the peoples.' We scarcely need the Bible to tell us this. Most of us have experiences similar to the two I have described. We have encountered a Jew here and a Jew there, always a minority, always somewhat apart, always a bit different. Some of us have seen the actual process of scattering take place, because it has never ceased for very long. We met some of the German, Austrian, Hungarian and Polish Jews Hitler's pogroms scattered in the 1930s; and it was only forty years previously that the scattering in Russia

115

brought into existence the Jewish population around the Whitechapel Road in East London.

The Jews are God's people. There is no denying this. The whole Old Testament is witness to the fact. And no one has ever been able to rub them out, and surely on no people has the effort been made as on this people to exterminate them, but they are with us still. Neither horrible persecution, inter-marriage nor religious apostasy has succeeded in obscuring, let alone obliterating, their identity. From the evidence of our eyes, nothing requires so easy a leap of faith as to believe that this people is *meant* to survive. God wants them to be, but he wants them *scattered* among the nations as an obvious minority.

It is not difficult for those of us who are Gentiles, and Christians among the Gentiles, to take only an academic interest in this apparent will of God that his people should be scattered, *until* the thought suddenly comes home to us that we too are God's people. Theologians speak of the Church as the New Israel. Is it true then that God wills that we too shall live as a minority group in the world? Apparently this is so.

Once again look around you. In Britain at the present time, even in areas where there is the greatest religious response among the public, only one in ten is a church-goer, and in the big cities only one in a hundred, in some places considerably less. Yet the fact is also observable that it is hard to find any place totally without any Christian witness. So Christians too are a scattered people. Ask even the youngest person with a lively faith. He/she finds himself/-herself in an office, in a factory, in a farming community, or goes into the army, is granted a place in the university, even stands in an unemployment dole queue. How lonely he/she feels at first, but sooner or later he/she discovers one other, perhaps two others, but only a minority, always only a little group of believers. God has his people scattered across the world, they are very thinly spread. So it always has been, and presumably always will be; which is why Jesus called his disciples leaven in the lump, and you do not need to be a *cordon bleu* to know that the amount of leaven (yeast) used in the making of bread is very small.

In 1980 the publishers Hodder and Stoughton brought out a book called *Life Sentence,* written by Charles Colson, who was President Nixon's 'hatchet man,' for which, after the Watergate scandal, he found himself in gaol. There his life was turned upside down, and he experienced a deep Christian conversion. When he had served his sentence, he said to his fellow prisoners. 'I'll never forget this stinking place and you guys.' Nor did he. He laboured hard to bring renewal, even Christian renewal, to those broken men, sticking to it through the inevitable derision that was heaped on him as a 'phoney do-gooder.'

Go where you will, into prisons, factories, colleges, schools, the armed forces, chambers of commerce, government offices, yes, and political parties, you will always find a little group of committed Christians. God has his people everywhere, but they are always thinly spread, they are always scattered.

2   God's reassembled people

Now let us return to the text again from Zechariah (scholars would wish to say Deutero-Zechariah). 'I have scattered them among the peoples, but from far away they will remember me (they will teach their sons, and these will return). I mean to bring them back . . .' It is the last sentence we need to notice. 'I mean to bring them back.'

If repeatedly in the Old Testament there is the threat of scattering, there is always by its side the promise of reassembling. The Jews aspire to this ingathering in the State of Israel, but the land can never accommodate more than a portion of the Jewish population. It can never be more than a symbol of an eschatological event (as we call it), an event in some far off future, indeed beyond time altogether.

And this certainly is how we Christians see the reassembling of God's people. Nowhere is this expressed more forcibly

117

than in the book of the Revelation, and nowhere more beautifully than in the Authorized Version set out in the Book of Common Prayer to be read on All Saints Day: 'After this I beheld, and lo, a great multitude, which no man could number, of all nations, and kindreds, and people, and tongues, stood before the throne, and before the Lamb, clothed with white robes, and palms in their hands; and cried with a loud voice, saying, Salvation to our God which sitteth upon the throne, and unto the Lamb. And all the angels stood round about the throne, and about the elders, and the four beasts, and fell before the throne on their faces, and worshipped God, saying, Amen; Blessing and glory, and wisdom, and thanksgiving, and honour, and power, and might, be unto God for ever and ever. Amen.'

This is the consummation, this is the reassembling of God's scattered people for which we await. The days of their minority will then be over.

3   Voluntary assemblies now

Thirdly, we ought to notice the phrase in the middle of these two verses from Zechariah. 'I have scattered them among the peoples, but from far away they will remember me.'

In the scattered experience with which all God's people live now, that is, before the great reassembling beyond time (what we have called the eschatological event), there are local and time-conditioned gatherings together. These are the Christian congregations, and among the Jews the synagogues; both 'congregation' and 'synagogue' have the same meaning—coming together, only one is Latin in origin and the other Greek.

This local coming together is vital. It sustains the life of those who otherwise might perish in the scattered condition of their experience. In the epistle to the Hebrews the author throws out this admonition coupled with a warning: 'We ought to see how each of us may best arouse others to love and active goodness, *not staying away from our meetings*, as some do, but rather encouraging one another...'

118

Churchgoing, assembling together in groups as Christian people, ought not however to be merely duty. It is a privilege. Georgi Vins in a book called *Three Generations of Suffering*, describes how, one evening, he observed his parents cutting up a small gospel into several parts and sewing it in sections into a coat collar, into the lining and into warm quilted trousers. This was Soviet Russia and they had been caught assembling with a handful of others for Christian worship. There would be no Bible to read in the labour camps beyond the Urals for which they were destined, and no opportunities for gathering together for worship or prayer.

Praying together is one of the privileges which the assembly of Christians makes possible, but there is also sharing in the hearing exercise of the Bible read aloud. It is one thing to study the Bible alone, it is another thing to sit or stand together in the presence of the Bible being read. When this ministry is taken seriously the word of God becomes living and active in a way that is not possible in isolation. The attentiveness of the assembly sharpens the attention of the individuals that comprise it, increasing receptiveness.

And there is singing. It is possible, it is on occasions even enjoyable, to sing in solitude, but to come into its own, singing must have an assembly, a group, a congregation. And if the Christian's faith does not at times produce in him the urge to sing, the reality of that faith is at least questionable.

I have left to the last the sacrament of the Lord's supper, the Holy Communion, the Eucharist. How is this possible in isolation? Surely the very existence of this central act of worship requires the coming together from time to time of God's scattered church people. Everyone who takes his Christian commitment seriously must make room in his life for what we may call 'table fellowship.'

Let me finish with this reminder. Whenever you see a church building, what you are really looking at is a place of promise; for, in the world as we know it now, believing men

119

and women are a scattered minority, but the Church designed and built for this meeting together from time to time points forward and outward and upward to the Great Beyond where God's people will be assembled by him in everlasting praise and joy. Of this the church building is a sign and a sacrament. Happy are the eyes which see it as such.

At the time of the seven hundredth anniversary of the founding of Salisbury Cathedral, there appeared these lines in the *Salisbury Gazette*:

> Faith dreamed you, lovely in aloofness, high
> Above the faltering whisperings of time;
> Faith built you, that to loftiness might climb
> The sobered thoughts of those who passed you by.
> Upheld in nothingness, a prayer, a sigh
> Of aspiration for a purer clime,
> All these are you, in artistry sublime
> Still thrusting upward to infinity.

Your church, our church, may not be Salisbury Cathedral, but its message is the same. Treasure it. Treasure the place where God's scattered people gather together now in the hope that they will be finally gathered together in eternity. Treasure it in practice.

25.   The Healing Sun

Malachi 4.2 (AV) *But unto you that fear my name shall the Sun of righteousness arise with healing in his wings.*

Some time ago I was told of a friend (who is Swiss and lives in Lucerne), that she had contracted an unpleasant skin disease seriously disfiguring her back. No woman would take this physical blemish lightly, and certainly not this lady. Of

120

course she sought a cure. And she obtained it—a complete cure. The treatment was simple and cost absolutely nothing. It was to go up to the flat roof of her house, strip and lie in the sun. Its rays did the rest.

1 A diseased Church

The last book in the Old Testament, the book called Malachi, brings to our attention a diseased Church, if not a dying Church. All the life had gone out of it since the revival instigated by Haggai and Zechariah, and there was little left but a mean, carping, critical, cantakerous community deeply divided; with the bored and blasé in the ascendancy and the devout huddled away in anxious pockets not daring to raise their voices.

The disease in the bloodstream of this Church manifested itself at certain specific points. One was the casual attitude to worship. Anything would do for the house of God. What would be counted disrespectful for the Persian civil overlord was reckoned more than adequate for the divine Lord of the universe. Truth to tell, worship had become hollow because God had become dead to them. Worship consisted in the boring observance of traditional actions to the accompaniment of meaningless mumblings. O what a weariness is in it! When can we escape to the golf course?

Another symptom was broken marriage. Everyone's marriage seemed to be 'on the rocks', so commonplace had the trek to the divorce court become. And what was worse, wives were being discarded for no better reason than that the girl next door possessed a more trim ankle, a better figure, or some money of her own. Never mind if she were of a different religious tradition or no religious tradition at all. Sexual satisfaction was the governing consideration. If religious principles were to be countenanced, and surely they were démodé, then they could only be second on the list of priorities.

And then the denial of the existence of any moral principle in the ordering of the world's life. The unscrupulous do

121

better than the honest, the 'smart alecs' grow richer than the trustworthy. So fiddling goes on apace, and why not? so long as the culprit is undiscovered. And whoever has muscle power, let him use it to his own advantage and that of his confederates. Never mind about injustices, so long as the consequences do not fall on one's own set. Whether we do good or whether we do ill, it all comes to the same in the end. No moral principles are at work in the world now, and there will be no divine judgement when we reach our end. Amorality, subtly camouflaged, pays.

And in this diseased and dying Church which the book called Malachi depicts, the priests have grown weary. They do not teach the people any more. Teaching is hard work. It requires preparation, it requires personality, it requires patience. Far easier simply to turn the handle of traditional ceremonial and let people make of it what they will, if they will. And anyway, religious enthusiasm is dangerous; visions and imagination can lead worshippers into all manner of excesses. Far safer to adhere to the cultus without deviation, and certainly far easier to find men able to fulfil this mechanical ministry.

2 A prophet for the times

Such was the diseased and dying Church to which this last prophet of the Old Testament was called to minister. It was a daunting situation in which to have to speak a word of God. Few audiences are more inhibiting than one that is bored and blasé. And we cannot in all honesty call this prophet a great prophet. What struggles must have raged within his heart and mind to dare to raise his voice in such a climate as this! But he was called to this ministry. He was labelled *Malachi* which means 'my messenger', God's messenger (for Malachi is not a proper name). And must we not believe that, minor prophet though he was, he was in fact fitted for such a situation as he faced. An Isaiah or Jeremiah would have been too great to make an impact, just as a voice, if it is too loud, cannot be heard.

122

My mind goes back only a few years when it fell to my responsibility to have to seek out and present a minister for a church some thousands of miles distant from Britain. The pastoral situation was a depressing one, being characterized by a dead formality and narrowness of vision. Even if there were the remotest possibility of appointing a theologian, an Oxbridge graduate or a revivalist preacher, it would have been a mistake. As it happened after weary months of painstaking search a late ordinand was found willing to undertake the work. He had spent a great part of his life plying a useful manual trade, was a humble and sincere Christian of upright life, and able to talk in homely terms to homely people. He sailed away and the last I heard of him was of excellent work being done, his handy hands proving to be his greatest asset.

No one must question the reality of Malachi's call to the ministry he exercised, nor fail to hear the word of God which fell from his lips. But it cannot be denied that there is no literary style about his utterances, nor any inspiring vision of God. He does not plead with his hearers, he argues with them. At one point he even plays on their hatred of the Edomites. And it could be thought that a return to correct ritual observances would in his view constitute the way out of the slough of useless religion into which his hearers had fallen.

We have to face the fact which the little ministry of Malachi forces on us that prophecy had failed in Israel. It had failed to bring the nation to God, loud and insistent though its call to repentance had been. The majority of the people did not, would not and therefore in the end, could not hear it. Was some other method called for? Is this the significance of the reforms of Nehemiah and Ezra, especially the latter? Did the Jewish backsliders from the life of faith need the discipline of law to effect the life style required of this covenant people? It was certainly tried and it achieved something. Let no one ever assent that law is *utterly* powerless to achieve good. This is not so. The law achieved a piety, but it was the piety of separation, a piety without

hope for the weak and sinful. Therein lay its weakness.
Therein lay the need for its surpassing.

3 The prophecy

All this is true, but we have not yet reached the justification
for Malachi's ministry which overtops all other justification.
It is found in his prophetic word and the little group of
faithful God-fearers hiding among the great mass of bored
and blasé people. 'But unto you that fear my name shall the
Sun of righteousness arise with healing in his wings.'

Go back to my opening illustration of my Swiss friend
exposing herself to the sun's rays to be cured of her skin
disease. In this diseased and dying Church to which Malachi
had been called to minister, we can be sure the general
malaise had not stayed from rubbing off even on the little
band of true God-fearers. What could heal this? What could
heal the great mass of this wayward people? More prophetic
utterance? It had done its work and failed! More stress on
cultic observance? It produced a pharisaic piety! There was
only one hope, but it was a sure hope. In due time the Sun
of righteousness would arise with healing in his wings.

The translators of the Authorized Version are to be
forgiven for writing Sun with a capital S. They saw, and saw
rightly, these words as pointing away to the Christ who
would come. The Persians under whose overlordship the
people of Malachi's time lived depicted the sun as an orb
with wings attached as a cultic symbol for God. Malachi saw
the Messiah under this symbolism. It was a true insight.
Healing comes through our willingness to expose ourselves
to this divine presence.

Is this outdated? No one with an open mind who listens,
for example, to the testimonies given by some of those who
form the congregation picked for the televised hymn-singing
programmes called *Songs of Praise* can think so. Clearly
these people have been healed by the Sun of righteousness
whom we know as Jesus the Christ. This is real. This is
practical. Malachi did indeed utter a genuine word of the

Lord which will not pass away. The Sun of righteousness *is risen* with healing in his wings.

26. Morning has Broken

Isaiah 60.1 (AV) *Arise, shine; for thy light is come, and the glory of the Lord is risen upon thee.*

On Sunday mornings at 6.30 there is a radio programme called *Morning has broken*, ending with a haunting Irish melody; and how haunting Irish melodies can be!

Morning has broken. Could any words be more fitting for some experiences than these? I think of the Russian Baptist pastor, Georgi Vins, arrested in 1974 for his preaching ministry and condemned for five years behind barbed wire, and then five years in a labour camp. The conditions were cruelly harsh as those who have read *The Gulag Archipelago* know. But suddenly, with no explanation from the Russians, on 29 April 1979, he found himself walking up the steps of the First Baptist Church in Washington DC with another Baptist, Jimmy Carter, President of the United States (who had worked so hard for his release). If the words, 'Morning has broken' fitted the experience of anyone, surely it was Georgi Vins that day in America. He could scarcely believe it, after the nightmare of the Russian slave camp with scarcely a hope even of survival.

1 The light of Isaiah's prophecy

The text from Isaiah 60.1 tells of a similar experience for a whole nation—'Arise, shine; for thy light is come, and the glory of the Lord is risen upon thee.' The exile, the captivity, the loneliness, the homelessness, the boredom, the drudgery, the depressing future is behind you. You are free from your chains, free to rebuild your life in the way you will, free to worship, free to speak your thoughts—'Arise, shine; for thy

light is come, and the glory of the Lord is risen upon thee.'
Morning has broken!

We in the Christian Church hear these Old Testament
scriptures with Christian ears, so that a conscious effort is
all but required to prevent us jumping straightway to their
application to Christ, especially if the stirring rendering of
this particular verse in Handel's Messiah rings in them.
'Arise, shine; for thy light is come, and the glory of the Lord
is risen upon thee.' But this is running too fast. First we must
absorb the historical situation as it was about the fourth
century BC to which this third part of the book of Isaiah
(where chapter 60 occurs), belongs.

Generally speaking, the population was depressed. True
the exile was decades behind them, but the tough problem
of rebuilding the homeland was proving to be much tougher
than expected. There were grumbles and quarrels, setbacks
and laziness. The nation seemed unable to pull itself
together. And nowhere did this feebleness show itself more
clearly than in Jerusalem itself, still half tumbled down. But
there was a voice, a prophetic voice, calling it to rise to its
freedom, calling to it, as if it were a woman prostrate on the
ground where she has lain all night. 'Arise, shine; for thy
light is come, and the glory of the Lord is risen upon thee.'
The picture is of the eastern dawn where the sun does not
gradually rise, diffusing the darkness with a kaleidoscope of
changing colours. It almost shoots above the horizon,
stretching out powerful shafts of light into every dark place.
'Arise, shine; for thy light is come, and the glory of the Lord
is risen upon thee.'

But did the people believe it? Alas, it seems they did not.
That is to say, morning or no morning, sunlight or no
sunlight, they did not arise out of their lethargy, they did not
work with a will, they did not gather together for worship
as if they believed in it, and in too many places social
injustice was fast creeping back through selfishness and
greed.

2   The light of Christ's birth

And so these dark and depressing days running into decades and much more than decades, dragged on, relieved only by the daring of the Maccabees in the second century BC. Then the dawn broke again, though it was thirty years before more than a handful recognized that the sun was up! 'Arise, shine; for thy light is come, and the glory of the Lord is risen upon thee.'

St Luke sets the scene in an outhouse with a baby cradled in a manger, born of Mary his mother. Of this child this same evangelist wrote, 'Through the tender mercy of our God: whereby the day-spring from on high hath visited us; To give light to them that sit in darkness, and in the shadow of death: and to guide our feet into the way of peace.'—Morning has broken!

The world is a different place now that Christ has been born in it. Tragedies look different. Opportunities look different. Even sins look different. Have you not gone through the experience of arriving at some place late at night? You look up at the house where you will be staying. It stands there gaunt and forbidding. And from the windows of your room the land appears to fall away into a veritable abyss. Then there are strange noises. There is a movement in the garden. Some clock chimes out the hour into an eerie stillness. You go to bed. You do not sleep well. But in the morning, when the sun is up, how different everything looks. The house is attractive, the landscape breathtakingly beautiful. And that clock belongs to a cathedral standing close by in all its grey stone beauty. 'Arise, shine; for thy light is come.' Morning has broken! So it is when we recognize that Christ is *in our world*. Problems remain; there is work to do; there are sins to be repented of and forgiven—but *it is light* and we can see. The light makes all the difference.

3   The light of Christ's resurrection

And then there came another dark day, when the heavens themselves with black clouds seemed to copy the black deed that men were perpetrating outside Jerusalem's city walls— the murder, the execution, the crucifixion of this same light of the world that was cradled in a manger. It was as if in some workshop where men and women were engaged on an intricate and beautiful piece of artistic construction requiring nimbleness of fingers and keenness of eyesight, let alone dedication of spirit, evil men marched in to extinguish the lights and black out the windows. Pitch darkness ensued in which the workers could only grope to find an exit, their work left unfinished, their hopes of completion dashed.

So it was that first Good Friday, but as the sun was shooting up from the eastern horizon, women and men (yes, in that order), knew that the light of Christ was not extinguished. The cross had not extinguished it. The grave had not extinguished it. Death had not extinguished it. Indeed, it burned all the brighter because man's last enemy had been conquered. Nothing now could blot out the light. The birth of Christ has changed our view of this world. The resurrection of Christ has changed our view of that which is to come.

4   The appeal

And so the appeal of this verse is made to us. 'Arise, shine.' Or in the words of St Paul to the Christians in Ephesus, 'Awake thou that sleepest, and arise from the dead, and Christ shall give thee light.' Or again, as in his address to the Romans, 'The night is far spent, the day is at hand: let us therefore cast off the works of darkness, and let us put on the armour of light. Let us walk honestly, as in the day; not in rioting and drunkenness, not in chambering and wantonness, not in strife and envying. But put ye on the Lord Jesus Christ, and make not provision for the flesh, to fulfil the lusts thereof.'

The Old Testament has told its story of God's encounter with man and man's encounter with God. There is light in that story and there is darkness in it. There is joy in that story and there is sorrow in it. There is success in that story and there is failure in it, and the failure in the end darkens the sky. This is the disappointment of the Old Testament. But then it happened. The light broke through in the darkest place, never to be extinguished. 'Arise, shine; for thy light is come, and the glory of the Lord is risen upon thee.' Christ is risen. Morning has broken. Alleluia!